Book Launch 101

Putting the Rockets on Your Launch Roll Out!

by Connie Dunn

Book Launch 101: Putting the Rockets on Your Launch Roll Out! © 2014 Connie Dunn

Published by Nature Woman Wisdom Press and Connie Dunn Books

First Edition. Printed and bound in the United States of America.

Published by Nature Woman Wisdom and Connie Dunn Books
Printed in The United States of America

ISBN-13: 9780615971346
ISBN-10: 0615971342

9 8 7 6 5 4 3 2

Library of Congress Cataloging in Publication Data

Dunn, Connie
Book Launch 101: Putting the Rockets on Your Launch Roll Out!

Book Marketing
        Book Launch 101: Putting the Rockets on Your Launch Roll Out!
        by Connie Dunn

Book Writing
        Book Launch 101: Putting the Rockets on Your Launch Roll Out!
        by Connie Dunn

C'mon
Let's
Launch

Table of Contents

It's Hard Work Launching a Book!

Does Anyone Know How to Attach Rockets to a Book?

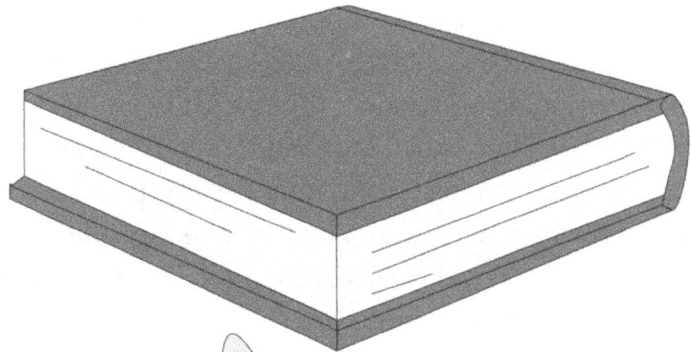

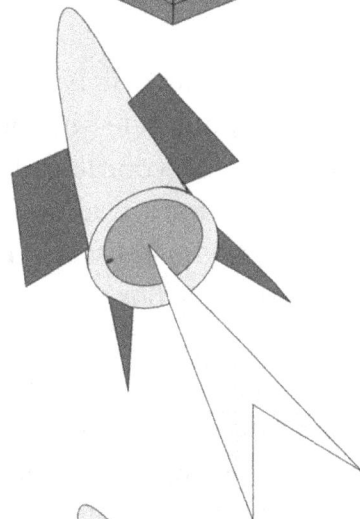

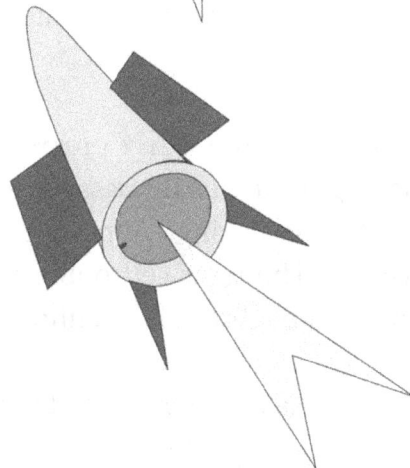

Overview

A launch can mean something different to different people. If you are published traditionally, the launch is the day the book arrives at bookstores. However, being independently published, the launch is a date you decide to launch your marketing for your book. For most independent publishers, the book arrives on Amazon quickly, depending on which on-demand print publishers. CreateSpace.com, for example, is an affiliate of Amazon and a book that is completed and approved appears within 24 hours on Amazon. For e-books on Kindle, less than 48 hours, the book is ready to sell. Nook and other e-book options are similar.

With traditional publishing, it is imperative that your launch take place quickly. As little as 10 days of poor sales in the book store, the store may ship it back to the distributor. At that point, your launch has fizzled. Developing your launch plan well in advance is mandatory for a traditionally published book. And unless you are as well-known as Lady Gaga, you are still in charge of marketing. There will be little or no help from the traditional publisher.

Perhaps, that is a very good reason for being an independent publisher. Or, perhaps, that you publish through an independent publisher, which is also possible. It has been my experience that being in control both creatively and financially, book publishing done your way affords you alternative ways to sell your book, and, occasionally, in traditional places.

While it really is not my purpose in this book to discuss the virtues of independent publishing, I can hardly pass over the topic. I, purposely, have not used self-publishing or vanity publishing, although these terms are often confused with independent publishing. The term self-publishing simply refers to you publishing your own book, which could be through a vanity press or through an independent publisher.

Vanity presses are more scam than honorable business. They prey on those who have a desire to publish, but naïve about the book publishing world. True, it is more and more difficult to get published traditionally. But there are more and more avenues to get published.

As an independently published author, you stay in control of all processes of your book. You do not hand over thousands of dollars to some press, who creates a book out of whatever it is that you send them. It may not look like the book that you intended, but that's because vanity publishers have not moved forward much like their traditional counterparts. Vanity publishers sell you a package that includes the whole enchilada, even if you'd really rather just buy the taco.

Independent publishers allow you to buy the taco or the whole enchilada, and anything in between. At the same time, you can arrange for all the same services that any of these publishers offer. Organizing the services of editors, book designers, cover artists, and marketing people may not be as difficult as you think.

The Internet and Skype provide a platform that literally connects you to anyone around the world. Sometimes you don't even have to look that far. Check within your local community to find suitable candidates. The Internet will offer every service you could need. But do not hire people without getting references. For artists, make sure you see their work before you hire. If you're on a budget, which most indie published authors are, check with your local high school or college art teachers for a good art student looking to make a few bucks!

When you hire your own people, you decide the rules by which they work. For example, in hiring an editor, you can tell them what you want them to do. If you want your editor to verify facts, they will charge you for that. If you have poetry in your book, you might not want them to edit the poems. You hire an editor; they work with your rules.

You will plan your own launch and marketing program. You don't have to market your book, but if you plan to sell any books, you will need to market it - that could be a totally online marketing plan or mostly in-person plan or a combination of the two. This is what works best for a lot of authors.

Local efforts surround small local bookstores. Online marketing can be comprehensive, such as a Virtual Blog/Book Tour, videos, e-mail marketing, Facebook marketing, and other online marketing tools.

What to Do Before Your Book Launch

Even before your book is completely finished, you can set up a Website and a Facebook Fan Page. On your Website, begin blogging. You can start with having your characters do your blog. Post announcements of tiny segments of your blog on Facebook and invite your readers to read the entire blog on your Website. Start an E-List and make sure to have your sign-up on your Website viewable for all your pages. You can easily do this by using the Widgets in WordPress. Choose the text widget and paste the code for your Sign-up form from your E-List manager, such as Aweber, Constant Contact, or MailChimp, into the text. This will appear on all pages, unless you choose a page to fill the entire space, which is an option on some WordPress themes.

Launch Parties

Launch parties are all about getting a good number of people to attend! While there may be more to do after the party, launching your book takes a bit of planning.

Your first task is to plan out the Launch! Let's back up just a bit and talk about what we mean when we say Launch and Launch Party. While they could be interchangeable, there arw also some differences that some people see. So...the party is a celebration. I think that's pretty clear. It's the "Launch" that could refer to the party, but it can also be when your book is available for sale or when you "launch" your book marketing program for this book.

Traditional, Self, or Indie?

From traditional publishers, when books are released to the bookstore, that is the "Book Launch." It is very important that you have organized all your marketing to launch at that point. Here's why: if your book should not sell during the first 10 days on the bookshelves, the book stores return the book to the distributors. So, you see, the launch of a traditionally published book must be planned well in advanced.

Vanity Presses, who work similar to Traditional Publishers in their services, do not have the same relationship with big box book stores. In fact, it's often the kiss of death to have a book done through a Vanity Press. Let me explain here that a Vanity Press has been the primary choice for self-published authors, because they offer all the same services that Traditional Publishers offer.

That said, you can be a self-published author without going through a Vanity Press. There has always been the choice of establishing an Independent Press, but it was not as easy as it is today. Independently owned publishing companies and on-demand printing has been a great marriage to offer more options. And with the onset of eBooks, the entire publishing industry has had a shift toward the Independent Publishing Industry.

Some of the options for Independent Publishing offer you the on-demand printing and fulfillment, as well as putting your book onto Amazon pretty immediately. These same companies also offer full services, but on an a la carte basis. Here's the litmus test for understanding how to determine if you are truly "Independently Published:" If you own the publishing or imprint name used for acquiring the ISBN, then you are an Independent Publisher.

You can do this easily through popular CreateSpace.com. This choice is an extra $10 for the ISBN. Interestingly enough, if you go directly to R.R. Bowker (myidentifiers.com) who manages the ISBNs in America, one ISBN number is $125 and 10 for $250.

Marketing Launch

A "Launch" for an Independent Publisher, is a lot more flexible. While your book is probably not going to sell well until you begin your marketing, you don't have the same urgency. Your book on Amazon is going to stay on Amazon, so you can set your own timetable.

Once your book is published, you need to move to the next phase: Marketing. The first phase is launching the book, which to many people means a launch party.

With traditionally published books that go into big box book stores, a launch might include organizing book signing opportunities in as many book stores as possible. However, one large launch party where you read an excerpt or whole book in the case of childrens' books, and do a book signing. Naturally, more book signings can be organized in various places, just think out of the box, as in out of the big box book stores. There are many independent book stores. These stores often feature local authors and host book signing parties.

The first thing you are going to have to do for your book launch party is to get people to come. You, naturally, want as many people as possible, including media. So…that's who you'll invite. The standard way to invite the press is through the use of a press release. Getting them to come to your party is probably not as important as getting them to interview you and write a story for their publication. For more information about how to write a press release, see the section on Press Releases.

There are a variety of ways to invite people to your Launch Party. You can send out e-mails and newsletters to everyone you know professionally (if appropriate) and socially. Another way is to send out invitations. In this electronic age, snail-mailed invitations might be more impressive. However, depending on your guest list, it is might have an impressive price tag, as well.

Facebook is a good place to put an invitation. It is preferred that you have established a Fan Page for your Book, see the section on Facebook, Website, and Social Media for more information on this. Posting an invitation on your Fan Page will be a good place for your fans to become aware of your book, this is especially true if this is not your first book. With multiple books instead of a Fan Page for your book, you might actually have an Author Fan Page.

Post a blog that invites all your blog readers and followers to your Launch Party. You want to get as many people at your party as possible. If your space is not large enough to accommodate everyone, make it a come-and-go affair. Make sure you have plenty of refreshments. Also send out e-mails to all your friends and ask them to forward your invite to others. It's a game of word of mouth that will get you a full house at your launch party. People who come will feel a bit of pressure to buy the book and get you to sign it, so higher numbers are always best. Some folks will simply come for the food.

Just like inviting your friends, send out blogs, e-mails, newsletters, etc. to any and all groups for which you belong. Ask them to put your info in their newsletter. You can even put up flyers where appropriate. If you book is a children's book for young children, say preschool age, see if you can distribute flyers to their parents. It is good to provide some activities if you are inviting children. Schedule your party so that it will be family friendly and be at a time that doesn't interfere with nap time.

Figure out the logistics of where people will sit to visit or if there should be standing room only. Try to think of all the things that would make your guests feel welcome. Make sure you have helpers around, so that you are not "doing" any of the "work." Your job, as author, is to enjoy your guests and sign books! Think of yourself as king or queen on this day! You deserve it. A book often takes longer than carrying a human baby to be born, so relax. You need time to recover from your labor pains!

Party Themes

Let's talk a bit more about organizing your party around a theme. While for some, having a launch party of any kind will be doing all they can, others may want to create a more elaborate party. Naturally, this is likely to add to the costs to your launch party.

Let's say that your book is a fantasy book for middle school, which is very popular with this age group. Naturally, your launch party will need to be marketed to this age group and their parents, librarians, teachers, etc. You'll want to deck out your launch party space to fit the theme of the book. Let's say your fantasy involves dragons, elves, and woods. Creating a wooded feel to your party space could be as easy as getting a florist to decorate for you. Or if you are on a smaller budget, you could create trees along the walls with a variety of arts and crafts material.

I once created a willow tree for a classroom out of a roll of brown paper with green crepe paper streamers. Be creative! You could also use felt, but that may be slightly more costly. Your characters could come to life with actors in costume or some friendly puppets. As a puppet creator, I always think of puppets first. Children relate to them easily and that is often better than characters in costume for small children. The decorations and characters in costume would work quite well for a second book, so that your young fans are already hooked. Letting them know ahead of time that their favorite characters will be at the party will almost surely bring in your fans!

Even non-fiction books can benefit from a themed launch party. You can go as elaborate as you can afford. Hire musicians and other performers, as appropriate. Some of the things that add to a party is to: have a good caterer to provide food, florists to decorate, and PR firms to promote your event for you.

The place for your Launch Party is also important and should accommodate all the people that you expect at your party. Your launch party is your celebration and should promote your book, even have books for sale so that you can sign them. But it is usually the beginning of your book marketing.

To put everything in perspective, create a marketing plan for your book with a Launch Party as a beginning. Tours for your book are primarily done virtually with the exception of local speaking engagements and library readings. Put a budget together to go along with your marketing plan. If you find that your budget is too high, go back through the budget and choose what is really not essential.

Launch parties can be very creative and decked out to match the theme of the book. However, a no-frills party can result in the same thing, so don't go elaborate for the sake of going elaborate, unless, of course, if you have unlimited funds.

Having money helps with a lot of things, but when it comes to taking your book on tour, you won't need it. Take your book on a virtual tour. After all, your book store, Amazon, and your Website are online!

FACEBOOK. . .

Yours or Mine?

Facebook, Website, and Social Media

Facebook

Facebook Fan Page

In the previous section, we mentioned that putting up a Facebook fan page for your book helps to promote the book and gather your fans. With social media growing, some Internet Marketing Specialists say that having a Facebook Fan Page may be more valuable than a Website. (Remember, however, that the Website holds your Blog and your signup form, so don't think you need an either-or can of choice.) Facebook Pages are easy to create. If you don't want this page to be connected to your private Facebook Page, you simply fill out the online information, answering the information with your book info. You do have to use your real name and birthdate as part of the informational process.

Facebook pages can be "liked," so you can do a "like" campaign. If you have a lot of books, you might set this page up as an "Author" page rather than the individual books.

Facebook and Pseudonym

However, if you are using a pseudonym, establishing your pseudonym might be as easy as setting that name up with its own Facebook page. Fill out as much of the background and employment information as makes sense. The birthdate should be your birthdate and other information should mirror your experience, such as if you are a school teacher, your pseudonym can be a school teacher. However, to keep yourself anonymous, don't use the name of your school, skip that information. Don't deliberately lie about things relating to yourself, but avoid adding information that is obviously fraudulent, because Facebook could close down your site. Just leave those questions blank! There are plenty of people on Facebook that have not entered any info.

The picture could just be an icon rather than an actual picture of you. Plenty of people have strange pictures up that represent them. For example, if your book involves dragons, you might upload a picture of a dragon to use as your picture. You should not have photos on your site, unless they are book covers or something related to your book. Keeping with the anonymity of your pseudonym means you cannot put info about yourself and family; therefore, cute pictures of your fur babies, children, grandchildren, etc. don't belong here. Set up a personal page for that.

Websites

Even though some experts feel that Facebook pages are more important than Websites, I feel that Websites can give all the information that you want people to know. Websites give much more information than a Facebook page can give. Connecting the two through links on your Facebook page posts can be very helpful. I think that Websites are more organized and easier to find important information, so I definitely would advise having a Website.

Information on your Website should be on "What's In It For Me/Your Reader" or as some people refer to is as favorite Radio Station WIIFM. When writing your bio or about page, it is good to state things in such a way that it gives more benefits than you might ordinarily use. Another way to think of it is why should someone listen to you?

You may be like me and be a bit shy about promoting yourself so blatantly. However, if you don't, then no one will know. I found stating it in a manner that explains why someone should listen to me changed how I wrote my credentials…in a way that shows my "benefits." In fact, I added things that I wouldn't ordinarily think of to tell people. For example, I won an award years ago for writing about small and home-based businesses…as a writing coach that becomes a benefit, because I obviously know how to write to relate to small and home-based businesses. I wrote my first independently published book in 1981…as a writing coach that's a benefit that lets potential clients know that I know first-hand about "independent publishing," because I've been doing it a long time.

Since WordPress has surfaced as one of the number one ways to set up a Website, the designing of Websites have become easier and easier. It is all word- or text-based. You really don't need to know any of the languages, such as Hyper Text Markup Language (HTML) or CSS, which is a more developed form of HTML.

I have been designing Websites since about the beginning of the Internet, and there has been a lot of change since then. I have found WordPress very easy and very difficult at the same time. When I want the page to look a certain way, it becomes a bit harder, because you may need to download and install a WordPress Plugin or find the html or css code to create certain things. However, learning that there is a table plugin has helped a great deal. I also recently learned about "Johnson Boxes," which are boxes that can be filled with color/shading. This, too, is a plugin. Now, instead of accepting the limitations that I felt WordPress had, I've found plugins to do just about anything. Changing themes can allow more flexibility, as well.

I will admit that there is a bit of a learning curve in using any of the plugins. However, putting in a plugin that automatically tweets your blog or posts to your Facebook page, makes social media easier and on automatic! There was little to learn about these plugins and a lot of "Wow! This is so cool!"

A "Book" or "Author" Website also needs some particular pages. The **Home Page**, of course, which could be a landing page or squeeze page or even a reposting of the most recent blog posts, is one page. You also need an **About the Author** page, a **Media** page, an **Events** page, a **Book Summary** (Summaries) page – one for each book if this is an **Author Website**. You also need to tell people how to buy your book on both your *home page* and *the book summary page*. A **Testimonial** or **Endorsement** page will show quotes and pictures of the people who have endorsed you, if you and your endorsee agree.

The **Media** page should have a photo of you in hi-resolution for print, your bio (I often just put a link to my bio page on the site), book summary, and any and all press releases, which I post all of them on my site with a link showing on this page. Anything that you want the media to know should go on this page.

The **Events** page is a page that shows where you are. It lists your book lunch and all other events, such as personal appearances and virtual appearances on other people's blogs (guest blog). This page should show all the places where you will be and the dates you will be there. The information on this page, should relate to the current book you are promoting with an archive for information about older books.

Use pictures, such as the cover of your book, place your picture on the **About the Author** page. Make your pages visually appealing. If you are totally lost on how to do this, you can hire this done.

White space on pages is also useful. You want to fill your pages with content, but remember that content should be "relevant content." Again, Website design and building the Website are easily hired out, if this is not your skill or one you want to acquire.

Social Media

Social Media includes Facebook, but has many more opportunities than just Facebook. One new option is Google+ with Google Hangouts. The "Hangouts" allow you to communicate with live video, pictures, and text. It offers the advantage of having a group of up to 10 people in a live video call.

According to 10WebTips.com, the top 10 Social Media for businesses are as follow:
1. LinkedIn.com
2. Twitter.com
3. Facebook.com
4. YouTube.com
5. Wikipedia.org
6. Technoratimedia.com
7. Digg.com
8. Upcoming.org
9. Answers.Yahoo.com
10. Yelp.com

While some of the above list is well-known social media sites, some on the list are not. Also, sites, such as YouTube, and Wikipedia may be very familiar as the repository for video or encyclopedia type information on a wide variety of topics. However, they may not be viewed as social media by many. Upcoming.com is a calendar and social media site that combines the two into listing upcoming events.

Technoratimedia is a site that has a search engine that collects, highlights, and distributes blog content. Digg, on the other hand, is a social media site featuring snippets of news material that people vote on. Answers.Yahoo.com is a social media site that allows users to post questions, as well as answer questions that are posted. Yelp has listings of businesses and other things, which allows visitors to post reviews.

The Buzz and the Launch

What is the buzz? The buzz is simply the posting on your blog, Facebook, twitter, and other social media sites, plus all the press releases that you send out with all the information about your book being available or will be available on a particular date.

Buzz happens as you talk about your book. It can be through print media, such an article in a newspaper or magazine or an online publication. The main thing is to keep trying to get the message out.

When you create buzz about your book, you basically don't want to leave any stone unturned. Friends and family are only one list of contacts that you need to make sure that you notify of your book. If you are in business, you may already have a list built. You'll need to keep that list informed about your new book, beginning with announcing that it is available and where it would be available.

Publishing Means You Are a Business!

Publishing a book actually means that you are in business! What do you need to do to become a business? First, you need to decide on a business name. There are several choices. Did you create your own independent publishing company name to use for the publisher of your book? If this is your choice, creating a formal structure like an LLC is good to protect your personal assets. At the very least, you need to register with your county registrar to protect your business name.

What are the business possibilities for your publishing company? You can be a sole owner or if you have a partner, you can be a partnership. What about incorporating? Creating your business as an LLC (Limited Liability Corporation) is a popular choice where one or more people are involved. Being an LLC restricts the personal liability and has been popular choice for Independent Presses or Publications. Members or owners can manage an LLC or hire a manager. LLCs may have a dissolution date. On the other hand, an S Corporation is another viable choice that also limits the liability. With an LLC, you may structure it so that you have officers, but it is not necessary.

Once you have decided what type of entity your business is going to be. You need to establish yourself as a business taking all the necessary steps to do so. Get an Employee

Identification Number, which is used instead of your social security number when you are an LLC or S Corporation, and even as a simple partnership.

Set up a bank account, accounting process, and start your business. If you setting up as an LLC for your Independent Press or Publication Company, which is recommended, then your next steps are mandated by your work as a Press.

Get an EIN (Employee Identification Number), even if you do not have employees. Register with RR Bowker at www.myidentifiers.com. Depending on your projected publication schedule for the number of books that you plan to publish, you can buy one ISBN (International Standard Book Number) number at $125 (current price in May, 2013) or 10 ISBNs for $250 or 100 ISBNs for $575 or even 1,000 ISBNs for $1,000.

Through the www.myidentifiers.com, you will manage your ISBNs assigning each number to a title and getting a barcode to display on your book. You will return to this site after you have completed your book and upload the printed version of your book as a .pdf. You will do the same for your cover. To learn more, go to www.myidentifiers.com and look for their instructions.

Now, you have come full circle again and need to create BUZZ for your book!

Build a list. How do you do that? First, create a report, eBook, or some other published work that you can give away as an incentive for signing up for your newsletter or e-mail list. It isn't enough to just create the incentive and set up a list and auto-responder for your free gift. You will need to drive traffic to your Webpage where people can sign up for your e-list.

Driving Traffic

What does *Driving Traffic* mean? The simple definition is anything that brings visitors to your page. You can do this in a lot of different ways.

First, you can advertise. But that carries a cost to it.

Posting a video with a link to a specific page on your site drives traffic, especially if the video goes viral. The link is called a "backlink," and Search Engines love these sorts of links. Each time you post on Facebook, make comments on someone else's blog, etc. this potentially brings you traffic.

SEO (Search Engine Optimization) is another way to drive traffic. This is the art of getting your Website to the top of Search Engines. The traffic then comes from being listed number one or on the first page, which will direct traffic to your page.

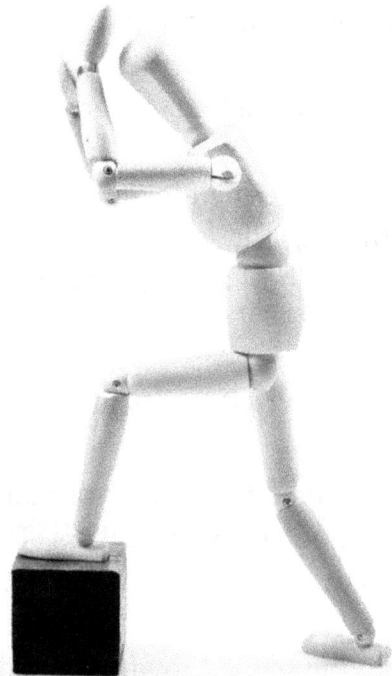

Get in
Shape
for
Launching!

10
11
How Many
Should I
Do?

Who to Invite to Your Book Launch

As above, we need to define what we mean by "Your Book Launch." In this case, we're going to say it is the "Book Launch Party." In this case, we're getting specific about a date, time and who to invite.

Naturally, you'd love the press to come. Send out press releases to the media with all the information: Who, What, Where, When, Why, and How. Although it would be nice if each publication would put this into their newspaper, it is highly unlikely. Therefore, you'll need to invite people in other ways, as well.

Let's go back to the question: Who to invite to your book launch? You will want as many people, as possible. But, in particular, you want people who will buy your book, because one of your main activities at this launch is "Book Signing."

Go back to your demographics and your definition of your best reader, who are they? These are the people you will want to invite. But where do you find them? If the socioeconomic group includes young adults in their 20s and early 30s, they will likely be hanging out on Facebook, LinkedIn, Twitter and other social media. Find out what social media that this group most likes and reach them there.

Send out e-mail invitations to special people, such as the Mayor of your town and other officials, if it seems appropriate to invite the dignitaries of your city. Invite the library staff of local and regional libraries.

Launch Party

Creating a theme for your launch that matches the theme of your book may help bring in some curiosity seekers. This could very intriguing, especially if you are a mystery writer.

Having helped my friend and student with her Launch Party, I must say this is the fun part of having gotten published. Planning a Launch Party is like planning any party, as far as refreshments. However, the goal is to sell books and sign books!

I've been pretty fortunate that my launch parties have been at a local bookstore, who plans the "party" part.

What a fun event! I'm not sure how many books that Helen Chin Lui sold of her first children's book, "Through My Mommy's Bellybutton" (to find out more about book or order book, go to www.throughmymommysbellybutton.com), but there was a good showing of people.

Launch parties are all about getting a good number of people to attend! Here's all the pre-planning that needs to be done:

- Send out Press Releases to all the local and regional media.
- Invite everyone on your e-mail list.
- Put an invitation on Facebook.
- Establish a Fan Page for your book, and put an invitation to your Launch Party on it, as well.
- Post a blog and send out an e-mail that focuses on your book and invites people to your Launch Party.
- Send e-mails to all your friends to invite them to attend.
- Send e-mails or send blogs or whatever is appropriate to any groups for which you belong, asking them to put your info into their newsletter, etc. Naturally, this is still inviting everyone to your Launch Party.
- Put up flyers where it is appropriate.
- Use just about any means of communication to invite people to your Launch Party.
- Your Launch Party should be scheduled for, at least, two hours.
- If your book is centered around families and you anticipate children at your event, there should be activities for them.
- If there are children's activities, make sure you have someone in charge of those, because, as the author, your job is to talk with all the attendees and sign books.
- Also, with invitations to families, you need to be sensitive to young children's schedules, such as an early afternoon nap.
- Now that you've invited everyone, make sure that your party place is spiffed and decorated, if appropriate.
- Figure out the logistics of where people will sit to visit or if there should be standing room only.

Try to think of all the things that would make your guests feel welcome. Make sure you have helpers around, so that you are not "doing" any of the "work." Your job, as author, is to enjoy your guests and sign books!

Think of yourself as king or queen on this day! You deserve it. A book often takes longer than carrying a human baby to be born, so relax. You need time to recover from your labor pains!

1. Matching Product Capabilities to Market Needs
2. Clear Positioning and Messaging
3. Setting Clear Launch Goals
4. The Power of Leverage
5. Priming the Pump
6. Timing the Launch to Maximize Sales

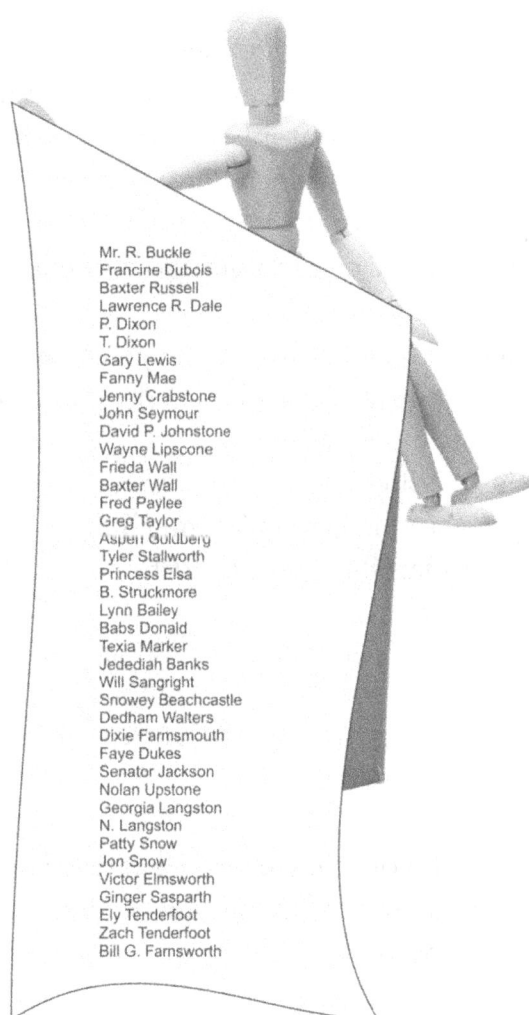

Mr. R. Buckle
Francine Dubois
Baxter Russell
Lawrence R. Dale
P. Dixon
T. Dixon
Gary Lewis
Fanny Mae
Jenny Crabstone
John Seymour
David P. Johnstone
Wayne Lipscone
Frieda Wall
Baxter Wall
Fred Paylee
Greg Taylor
Aspen Guldberg
Tyler Stallworth
Princess Elsa
B. Struckmore
Lynn Bailey
Babs Donald
Texia Marker
Jedediah Banks
Will Sangright
Snowey Beachcastle
Dedham Walters
Dixie Farmsmouth
Faye Dukes
Senator Jackson
Nolan Upstone
Georgia Langston
N. Langston
Patty Snow
Jon Snow
Victor Elmsworth
Ginger Sasparth
Ely Tenderfoot
Zach Tenderfoot
Bill G. Farnsworth

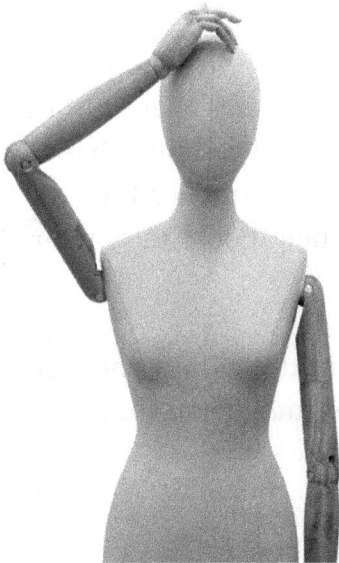

Press Releases

Writing a press release to announce your newly published book is always a good idea. And if you are launching your book with a party and book signing, add that to your Press Release.

Press releases are meant for the masses, the general public. It is a mass communication piece. As such, while you have a smaller audience to appeal to that is your niche market, this is one of those times when you have to step out of the niche and into the mass of generality.

Although a press release does not target a niche, because newspapers are a mass communication outlet, you can also send the same press release to more targeted newspapers, magazines, and newsletters that do target your more narrowly focused book audience.

How Do You Write a Press Release?

Every Press Release needs to answer: Who, What, Where, When, Why, and How. But to do this in a creative method that catches your audience and draws them through the News Release (note that a News Release and a Press Release are used interchangeably), you need to carefully craft your words. Each paragraph should lead to the next paragraph. If you want people to feel excited about your new book, then your Press Release should reflect that mood.

A Press Release can be written on your letterhead paper, but these days, more releases are sent via e-mail than by snail mail. These are the standard things you should have on your Press Release:

- The *Date* should go on the left-hand side of the page.

- The *Contact Information* should go on the right-hand side of the page. Give as much contact information as possible, such as the person to contact (this is especially important if you have a publicist handling some of your publicity), their address, phone (including a Cell phone), fax (if you have one), email and Website address. You want the media to be able to contact you, so help them do their jobs. When you send a Press Release to the media (newspapers, magazines, television, and radio), you want them to contact you. You are hoping for an interview that will lead to an article or maybe a guest appearance on radio or television.

- The *Release Date* is centered and should be in all caps. If you are ready to release when you send out your Press Release, use: FOR IMMEDIATE RELEASE.

- The purpose of your Press Release is to promote your book, so your *Headline* should reflect that. This line goes under your Release Date. The *Headline* should be larger type than the body of the News Release, centered, but not all in caps. Your Headline is important to get the attention of those who will read it, but it is rarely the headline that goes into an article.

The Body of Your Press Release:

Your first 10 words are the most effective and powerful words you will write. Since this is all about marketing, what you really want to establish in your *Hook* is what the *Problem* is that your book *Solves*. Refrain from using big, flowery or fancy language. Use real facts and attribute those to their sources. If your book is a work of fiction, focus on the topic for which your book deals.

Quotes within your Press Release are good and can be your own words or a testimonial by someone else or both. If you are having a launch event or even a virtual tour event, make sure you include all the details, such as where it will be held (address), when it is happening (day and time), who is invited. Event details should actually come at the top of your Press Release.

(See SAMPLE Press Release on next page.)

Sample Press/News Release

December 23, 2011

CONTACT INFORMATION
Connie Dunn
110 Dean Ave.
Franklin, MA 02038
508-520-3457 * CELL 508-446-1711
connie_dunn@hotmail.com

FOR IMMEDIATE RELEASE

WANT TO WRITE A BOOK?

Are you one of the hundreds of people who want to write a book, but just haven't quite gotten to this project. Well, what are you waiting for? You could have something very important to the world locked away in that brain of yours. If you don't get it written down, it'll be lost.

Nature Woman Wisdom is starting two writing groups in January. A woman's writing group that is being co-sponsored by the Dream Factory, a community of entrepreneurial women who want to realize their professional dreams. This group will be meeting once a month face-to-face for two hours on the second Thursday of each month.

The second group will meet twice a month on the first and third Tuesdays via teleconference and is open to men and women. Because this is a teleconference people can be located virtually anywhere. This is also only an hour at a time, so that people can more easily fit it into their busy schedules.

This group will take writers wherever they are in the writing process and help them get manuscripts ready for publishing. For more information, contact Connie Dunn at connie_dunn@hotmail.com or 508-446-1711.

Virtual Book Tour

What is a Virtual Book Tour? Just what you might think! Instead of flying around the world to promote your book, you can sit right in your living room and tour virtually, online. Here's how it works: take the topic of your book, and then find blogs that are written about that topic and ask to be a guest blogger.

It sounds fairly simple, right? Well, before you start cheering, let me tell you the down side. You need to develop a relationship with the owner of the blogs that you wish to tour. This is not rocket science, but it is good relationship marketing.

Would you buy a car from someone who comes to your door and makes a pitch to sell you the car? Probably not! You want some level of comfort with the person from which you purchase a motor vehicle. You are not selling a car, but you are selling yourself to the blog owner, who needs to feel comfortable turning over their podium to you.

There are more than 66 million bloggers (as of May, 2013) around the world. There is a good chance that there are plenty of bloggers blogging on the topic of your book. You can ask to be a Guest Blogger. But before you do that, make sure you spend some time visiting and commenting on the blog. This does several things for you:
1. Builds a relationship with a fellow blogger;
2. Helps you understand the audience of the blog;
3. Makes you a familiar post on the blog, which will help when you are actually guest blogging on the blog.
4. Gives you a back link to your Website.

You can stretch your topic to fit into a lot of different Blogs. For example, I toured with *Press Releases Made Easy*, and I visited a wide variety of blogs. For a

Many people want to skip the step of building a relationship, but it is too important to just jump into requesting to post a guest post without building the relationship. It doesn't really take long to build a relationship. They will see your e-mail address on posts and will soon know you by your e-mail. Drop a line to them on Facebook or by e-mail to start a friendly chat. Then ask about their hosting of your guest column. Once the relationship has been made, it is far easier to write your blog post directed to the audience of the guest blog.

Once you have found blogs, made a relationship with the blog owners, gotten permission to be a guest blogger on the blogs, then you need to schedule out your guest blogs. The guest blog posts serve as a virtual book tour. When scheduling these guest blogs, make these posts fit into a one to three week period.

The idea is that you schedule your blog tour for one to three weeks. Concentrating your posts during this particular time frame equates the traditional book tour that launches a book through guest appearances at book stores around the country. Instead, you can have a virtual book tour that spans the world. Since most "Independently Published Books" are sold on Amazon.com, which is the world's largest book store that happens to be online or a virtual store.

This type of book tour takes a bit of time to organize, schedule, and then deliver on the blogs. While we have discussed finding blogs that match the topic of your book, we have yet to discuss other appropriate blogs to target. If you are in business, there may be other blogs that would be appropriate for guest blog posts, such as those that have more to do with your business. If your business has more than one topic option, go for all of them that you can.

Guest Blog Posts

When you write a Guest Blog, it shouldn't be a sales pitch for your book. Instead, the blog post should be an article about the topic that goes with the blog for whom you are guest posting. For example, let's say your book is about *gardening*, but your business is about *holistic herbal medicine* and *Reiki energy medicine*. Your guest blogs can be on blog sites with topics that cover:

- gardening,
- herbal gardening,
- herbal medicine, and
- Reiki energy medicine.

Once you have determined the blogs for which you will appear as guest blogger, you will need to not only schedule your guest blogs but also write the blogs. Don't underestimate the value of writing superior blog posts for your guest blogging opportunities. Putting your best foot forward is always a good idea. After all, you've asked to be a guest on their blog, so make sure their hospitality is well-paced!

Many authors and entrepreneurs have virtual assistants. It is possible to deligate some of the process of finding the blogs, scheduling, and posting the blogs. Obviously, you will have to write your own blogs. But as busy entrepreneurs, it is always a good idea to take advantage of all your resources.

Organizing your tour takes time, energy, and scheduling. Having an assistant who will coordinate your blog tour for you is invaluable. After you have written your blogs your assistant can arrange to post the blogs at appointed time, according to your schedule.

If you must do this on your own, plan your tour so that you have time to write all of your blog posts up front. Send your blogs to your hosts a couple of days before they are to run is a good idea. Sending them as much as a week ahead, works for some hosts. I did run into some technically challenged hosts where the post did not appear as scheduled. But it gave me an opportunity to assist and even teach something to my host.

Virtual Review Tours and Press Kits

Another type of Virtual Book Tour involves getting your book reviewed. Book reviewers naturally require a copy of your book to read. However, when sending out a copy of the book, it's a good idea to also send a press kit or media kit. The press/media kit usually has:
- Press Release – sometimes more than one to show different perspectives from which you can promote;
- Page with all your media information in one place;
- Page with links to previous media coverage that you have already received;
- Page with facts about your industry and/or book topic;
- Page, listing topics for which you can speak or write about, and suggested angles for feature stories about you;
- Pre-written stories about you and/or your book;
- Questions for interviewing;
- Photo of you, the author;
- If possible, you can also include short audio and video clips of you being interviewed; and
- Book video/audio trailer, if you have one.

While Press Packets are "old school" or prior to e-mail and the Internet took preference for most things, the information is the same. The delivery, on the other hand, can be done simply by creating a Media Page on your Website and putting the above list on the page or a link on the page. Instead of sending formal letters, we now e-mail. Therefore, you can give them the link to your Media Page with all the information they need.

Most of the Book Reviewers are Bloggers. There are literally hundreds of Book Review Blogs on the Internet. Each Blogger has a particular genre that they choose to review. It is fairly easy to find a book reviewer for any genre.

Extended/On-Going Tour

An Extended or On-Going Tour is when you do a guest blog maybe once a month. This is particular advantageous for non-fiction writers, and for entrepreneurs who have written their book to promote their expertise.

Authors who have multiple books might also choose this sort of tour. Authors can promote individual books or themselves as an author. Guest Blogs as an author might speak to the genre that they write. Be creative in the way you organize an on-going author tour.

Other Virtual Tours

The Launch Tour is the primary type of tour; however, the Social Media Tour is a popular tour, which involves stops on blogs, podcasts and online radio shows. These Tours normally happen at launch or shortly after your book launch. However, you can promote your book at any time in this manner.

When you have a book that is printed by an on-demand printer and on Amazon, your book never goes out-of-print. Therefore, you need to continue to promote your book. It's good to plan out a yearly promotion plan for each of your books. For example, if you have a book that appeals to mothers of any age, then do a campaign just before Mother's Day every year.

Find a good time to promote each of your books and regularly promote each of them!

Amazon Best Seller Campaign

Another way to promote your book is to do an Amazon Best Seller Campaign. This entails getting people to buy your book on a particular date, which hopefully puts you on the Amazon Best Seller list. You can combine this type of campaign with your standard Launch or Virtual Book Tour.

Although the Amazon Best Seller Campaign sounds like a great idea, don't underestimate the work it requires. For it to be successful, it needs to be organized down to the tiniest detail. You're going to need to reach as many people as possible, using all social media avenues, as well as guest blogs and e-mails.

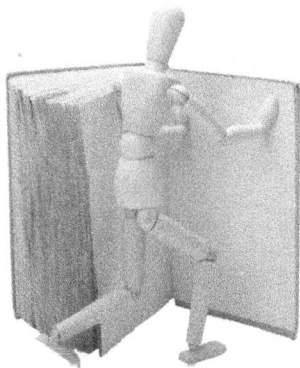

Let's see. . .
Optiming Readers. . .
.Hmmmmmmmmmmmmmmmm!

Optimizing Your Readers

Building an eList of your Readers is difficult when you first begin. It's sort of the question about "What came first, the chicken or the egg?" Does your list come before the book is published? Do the readers happen before the book?

Good questions…and, yes, these are a dilemma. If the book isn't out, how can you have readers? Well, to begin with, you do have to give something to get something. Create a give-away that has something to do with the topic of your book, yet not in your book. Promise to advise when the book is out. Use the site to pre-sell your books.

Building an eList

In "The Field of Dreams," a famous line was: "Build It and They Will Come." Not so much with eLists. You can put up an Opt-in Form on your Website and on your Blogs and correspondence, but unless you're giving away something of value, people are not likely to sign up. They want to make sure they will get something of value to them. It is again our old friend WIIFM! Make sure what you give away will attract your readers. If your books have widely different audiences, you might think about giving away more than one free product.

Now, here's what many successful entrepreneurs are doing: they are putting their opt-in forms on Facebook. They may also be pulling in their Blogs and Sales Pages, as well. This would all fall under the general category of Facebook Marketing.

Opt-In Give-Always need to be content heavy. These reports or eBooks shouldn't give up all your tricks and tips. In spite of this sort of limitation, eBooks do need to give hiqh quality content.

Adding an Opt-in App on your Facebook Page (Book or Author Page) can help build your list. Adding an Opt-in App is not terribly difficult. If you are using AWeber.com as your auto responder and list manager, then go to AWeber, click on the "MY APPS" button at the very top of the screen and follow the directions given. If you use AWeber for more than one account, repeat the steps for each page or whatever AWeber has posted. Facebook makes changes and AWeber updates their directions accordingly.

Shortstack.com also helps you design apps for Facebook. Opt-in Forms for MailChimp, for example, can be done in Shortstack. You can design many other types of apps, including entire pages that open in Facebook. These pages can be on your website that get pulled into an app or an entirely different ones that you use just on Facebook.

Facebook Marketing

Facebook Marketing is another marketing medium that requires some thought and strategy just like your Website. Take a bit of time to develop your strategy before immersing yourself in creating content for Facebook. It will be beneficial down the line to have all your strategies written out so that you can determine what works and doesn't work. From a marketing standpoint, you always want to have strategies with measurable outcomes.

Adding a Blog to Lure Readers

Because people's tendencies are not to give anything without a return, add a blog to your book or author site. Blogs give people a reason for coming to your site, even before your book is published.

Blogs should be written with keywords in mind. It works well to make a list of the keywords before writing your blog, then work in the keywords to your blog. At least, one keyword should be used in the first sentence.

Pick a Word Press Theme that you can customize and add your own logo, if not the entire headline. Colors and typeface are also able to be customized. Create a unique blog visually, but more than just making it unique "Brand It!"

If you already have a business, create a Book Website that has similar colors, etc. That way, you get the most mileage out of everything you do. If you have several books, then create an "Author Site" to promote your books and yourself in the process.

If you don't have a business and you are publishing your books as your own "Independent Publisher," then you are in business. Your business is publishing your books. Actually, if you have published a book, at all, you are in business! Your business is the book or books that you have published. If you publish under a particular publishing name, then set up a Website and a Facebook Fan Page to reflect the Publishing Name.

Create a "Feed Button," "Share Button," and "Forward Button." Write shorter paragraphs, so that people can better digest your writing. Run the spellcheck, so that you don't have misspelled words all over your blog.

Building Community; Building Content

Build your "Reader Community" through content marketing, which is giving your readers the information that they want. The topic of your book and the content you provide in your blog is important, but more than that, you need to be passionate about the content you are providing.

There are a lot of ways to optimize your readers, but the one that makes the most sense must be the one that speaks to you, as well. Since each person's reasons for writing may be different, the motivation behind your writing may help you figure out how to optimize your readers.

Bring all the pieces of what you do together, such as your business, other books you've written, your publishing (for those who publish under their own independent publisher or imprint [name]) business. Decide what makes sense marketing-wise. How do all of these pieces fit together? Optimize your readers for your book(s) through content and relationship marketing.

Content Marketing is enticing people to come to your Website based on the content that you offer. This works best if all the content is focused on a topic. You could have a combined site with all your business and publishing interests on the same site with a blog that focuses on the topic. However, everything on your Website needs to focus on the same topic or you muddy the content.

Creating a community also means you need to build relationships with your readers. You do that by giving them the opportunity to indulge in a discussion about the topic of your Website. Communities can extend their conversations on social media sites like the new Google Hangout.

Another way to gain readers is to create a good newsletter with options to forward. Newsletters on their own are not enticing enough to get people to sign up for your eList. However, combine a good newsletter, good Web content, superior blogs, and an attractive give-away to grow your eList.

Book Tour Blogs and Schedule

The information in this chapter is taken directly from my Virtual Book Tour for "Press Releases Made Easy." What I hope you glean from this chapter is how to do the nuts and bolts of a Virtual Book Tour. I have included a blank form in the next Resource Chapter, which will allow you to schedule the same way that I did.

This is how I filled out my Scheduling Form. Note the "Check Marks" that are there to notate written, then delivered. It allowed me to visually see what I had completed and what needed to be done. I did not do a Scheduling Form for the Blogs on my own site.

(See the Next Page for SCHEDULING FORM)

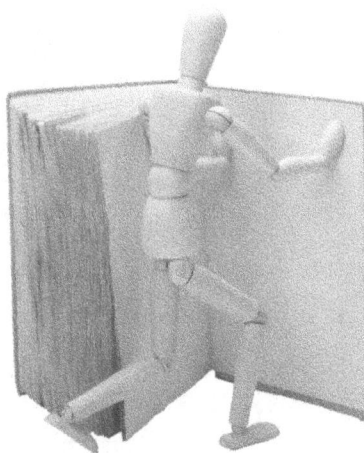

Schedule? I think it's in here somewhere!

Title of Book/Project

Day of Tour	Web URL	Purpose of Contact	Name of Person	Resolution	Date of Blog Post	Blog Title
1	www.dreamfactorycommunity.com	Req. Guest Blog Host	Nancy Cantor☑ 27 Tri Street · Ashland, MA 01721-2023	YES	July 1	How a Community can Support a VBT ☑☑
2 *	http://digitalpublishingcafe.com/virtual-book-tour-celebration-of-connie-dunn-author-of-press-releases-made-easy/		Dvorah Lansky	YES	July 2	Hall of Fame ☑☑
3☑	http://www.healingplacemedfield.com/helen-chin-lui-certified-reflexologist-blogs		Helen Chin Lui☑ **50 North Street, Medfield, Massachusetts USA 02052.**	YES	July 3	Heart Chakra and Book Writing ☑☑
4 *	Publishwithconnie.com/blog		Connie Dunn	N/A	July 4	Using Press Releases to Kick off Your Book Marketing ☑☑
5☑☑	http://etiquettefortoday.net/blog/		Janet Parnes☑	YES	July 5	Etiquette of VBT ☑☑
6☑☑	http://www.executivecoachingbusinessblog.com/		Ed McDonough☑ 869 Main Street - Suite 1 - Walpole, MA 02081	YES	July 6	Book Marketing Using Blogs and Press Releases ☑☑

#	URL	Contact		Date	Title
13☑	http://savvymarketingsecrets.com/blog/	Marcia Ming		July 13	Press Releases: Marketing Secret Still Good in the Digital World ☑☑
14☑	http://writingandeditingtoday.com/blog/	Gina Akao 3240 Alpine Creek Rd. Reno, NV 89519	YES	July 14	Editing Is An Important Step in the Publishing Process☑
15☑	http://www.organizingbykazia.com/blog	Kazia Navas kazia.navas@gmail.com 774.217.1779	YES	July 15	Organizing Is More that a State of Mind ☑☑
16☑	http://www.savvyvirtuals.co/bookmarketing/blog/	Eunice Nisbett info@savvyvirtuals.com P O Box 1525 Basseterre St Kitts W1001	YES	July 16	Why Do Authors Need to Learn about Press Releases, Blogs, and Web Design?☑
17☑	http://barbarawassermancoaching.com	Barbara Wasserman	YES	July 17	Re-writing Your Life Story☑
18☑	http://www.successcoachingwithkate.com/blog/ :	Kate Breeders 5056 Broadlawn Park #31Chestnut Hill, MA 02467	YES	July 18	The Three Top Reasons for Successful Businesses to Write a Book☑☑
19 *	http://www.soma1320.com	SoMa 1320 A.M. Soma Broadcasting P.O. Box 1321 Attleboro, MA 02703		July 19	MY RADIO INTERVIEW with Domenic

20 ☑ ☑	http://www.castlevirtualsolution s.com/blog/	Lorraine Castle P.O. Box 3807 Cherry Hill, NJ 08034	YES	July 20	Delegating Is an Essential Tool for a Writer ☑ ☑
21 *	http://www.conniedunnbooks.c om	Connie Dunn	N/A	July 21	The Virtual Book Tour (wrap up)

Notice the check boxes on these three pages!

The check boxes are a way to denote jobs done for each guest blog. The check boxes in the field for the Blog Title let me know that the blog was written and then sent to the blog host.

The check boxes in the day column told me that Thank You notes were written and sent.

There is a Blank Form on the next page. Copy and paste it in a file for yourself and begin filling it in. You'll notice that I had 21 Tour Dates, but the number of days can be whatever works for you.

One author that I know took a Tour from April to August, doing two or three days a week. Another did 10 days straight. Others have done a full 21 days, which is a three-week tour, or 15 days, which is also a three-week tour.

My Tour Stops included Blogs, Amazon Author Central, a Radio Station where I was interviewed, and my own blogs: ConnieDunnBooks.com and PublishwithConnie.com.

Title of Book/Project

Date	Web URL	Purpose of Contact	Name of Person	Resolution	Date of Blog Tour	Blog Title

Guest Blogs for Tour July 1-21, 2013

DAY 1 - HOW A COMMUNITY CAN SUPPORT A VIRTUAL BOOK TOUR
Guest Blog
by Connie Dunn

First, you may be wondering what a "Virtual Book Tour" is? In the past, book authors would travel around the country, speaking, reading excerpts of their book, and signing books. Most of that would happen at the big box bookstores. In today's virtual world, however, more book tours are taking place on the Internet, especially those independently published.

Since the tour takes place on the Internet, it is done through "Guest Blogs." Perhaps, you now understand where the "Community" part comes in. To tour, you need to visit blogs. While touring with a book, it might seem natural to want to post on blogs that match the book topic. However, it is not necessary that every Blog match perfectly. The signature on the Guest Blog is the part that promotes the book and has a link back to the book's page.

Authors pick blogs to tour that they can write articles that fit with the topic of the blog. For example, recently Helen Chin Lui published a children's book, "Through My Mommy's Bellybutton". Her book is written from the point of view of the baby in the belly, so her tour blog might include parenting blogs, moms-to-be blogs, or even fertility blogs. Since Helen is a Reflexologist and Energy Medicine Practitioner, she might also write articles for holistic healing blogs.

My tour is to promote my book, "Press Releases Made Easy." I will want to tour on marketing and public relations-type blogs, as well as many others. As a writer, you can connect a lot of things to a book topic without directly relating to the book. As I suggested with Helen's tour, she can tour other holistic healing bogs.

As a writer, I can tour other writers' blogs, plus a whole lot more! It's going to be an adventure and today is the first day! So come along with me and visit some parts of the Web you haven't ever seen!

Signature----------- (Note: This signature was added to each post, although it does not show on each one in this listing of blogs.)

Connie Dunn is taking a Virtual Book Tour promoting "Press Release Made Easy" (www.conniedunnbooks.com/books/press-releases-made-easy) visit her Blog at www.conniedunnbooks.com/blog/ or Events Page at www.conniedunnbooks.com/events/ . Follow Connie on her tour from July 1-21. On the 21st, a Trivia Quiz will be posted to her Blogl Prizes will be awarded for the first six people. For details see www.conniedunnbooks.com/events/trivia-contest/

DAY 2 Took visitors to a page where I was honored in the *Virtual Book Tour Hall of Fame*, and showed my *Celebrity Author Status*.

DAY 3 - HEART CHAKRA AND BOOK WRITING
Guest Blog
by Connie Dunn

Hello Healing Place Medfield followers. I have had the opportunity to meet a few of you, and so many of you will know that I am both a book writer, as well as a teacher for getting your book written and published.

However, today, I want to introduce you to the idea of writing from your heart chakra. This is not something brand new, because many people have written about heart-centered writing.

To get yourself into the right frame of mind before you begin writing, get quiet and centered. Put your feet flat on the floor, your back straight, allowing you to breathe deep. Take three deep breaths and let them out slowly. Then focus your attention on your heart chakra, which is right at the breast bone area. The color of the heart chakra is green or pink. You can close your eyes and see if these colors play around in your brain. When you are ready, you can gradually become aware of your surroundings.

Now, you are ready to write, because now you are focused on your heart chakra. Naturally, writing tends to take you out of the heart chakra and up to your throat chakra, which is your communications chakra. You should do this before your bring out your writing gear. Write via computer or by hand in a spiral notebook.

You've focused yourself, so don't push yourself to write for writing sake. Instead, relax and trust the universe to provide you with inspiration. Because this is a new experience, you may have a bit of difficulty with just trusting the universe. Perhaps, you are not aware of all the ways in which the mystery of the universe, which some people would call God, actually works. But this is unnecessary for the purpose of allowing Divine guidance into your writing.

Stay quiet for up to 30 minutes. If the muse has not touched your heart, perhaps there is nothing you need to write today. Don't give up on this, if you do this every day for a week, you will find what touches your heart to write.

You'll be amazed at the power of the universe to guide you into creativity. Writing becomes more like downloading than struggling with writing.

DAY 4 –USING PRESS RELEASES TO KICK OFF YOUR BOOK MARKETING
Blog – Publish with Connie
by Connie Dunn

When you begin marketing your book, it would be easy to overlook a method that has been used as a way of announcing an event since newspapers came into being: the Press Release. In this new technology driven world in which we live, the Press Release is not dead. It is a vital part of the "Kick Off" of a book marketing plan.

As the first thing that you send out, the Press Release should explain what a Virtual Book Tour is, because most people don't know what it is. The Virtual Book Tour is the primary way to market a book in this new virtual world in which we live. This means the marketing is all online or on the Internet.

Book marketing is now something that every author needs to do, whether you are traditionally published, indie published, or self-published. While this article is not about the manner in which a book is published, it should be noted that even the traditional or big book publishers no longer provide marketing as part of their book package, unless you are as well-known as Lady Gaga or Martha Stewart.

Of course, this means that every author needs to know how to write a Press Release. Naturally, if you personally have deep pockets, you can just hire everything done. Publicists normally view self-promotion as a "kiss of death" for your book. However, there are many people, especially, indie published authors, who would rather stay in control. Self-promotion may be viewed in a negative light by some. Others find it fun. Actually, who better to promote a book than the person who will benefit the most!

When writing your Press Release, do your research. The who, what, where, why, when, and how are standard pieces of a Press Release, but there are many other techniques that you can use to punch up your Release that helps grab the attention of the person reading it. Post your Press Release to your Website with a link to it on your Media page.

DAY 5 – ETIQUETTE OF A VIRTUAL BOOK TOUR
Guest Blog
by Connie Dunn

Before understanding the etiquette of a Virtual Book Tour, you will need to understand what a Virtual Book Tour is. I have to say that while this is a relatively new marketing tool for me, it appears to be one of the most intriguing endeavors I've undertaken. It is a tour of different blogs all over the Internet for the purpose of promoting my new book, "Press Releases Made Easy."

Like all business relationships, there is a certain decorum expected. When business people appear in person, then there is an expectation that they look the part. There is also a certain air of intentionality set when one dresses the part they hope to be. While I am not appearing before you in person, there is some expectation that what I write here will be useful to you at some point.

Marketing has vastly changed over the years. An author used to travel the country appearing in bookstores to read an excerpt of their book and sign books. While that was a way to get in front of readers, now you can do that from the comforts of your living room. At the same time, etiquette has not really changed!

The way Virtual Book Tours work is that you get to write a blog that will appear on someone else's blog. This sort of relationship deserves the right kind treatment. While a lot of communications is done via e-mail, thank you notes should be done through snail mail with a hand-written envelope. There are two opportunities to send these out. Once your host accepts you as a guest blogger and once you've appeared on their blog. Each of these opportunities deserves your best relationship building by sending a "Thank You Card."

DAY 6 – BOOK MARKETING USING BLOGS AND PRESS RELEASES
Guest Blog
by Connie Dunn

"Book Marketing" is a far cry from rocket science, but the "marketing" word can often be a bit as scary for some authors. Although writing is a big part of marketing, it is different from writing a book. However, some pieces of book marketing are not so foreign.

Blogs are simply articles that are usually focused on your "niche" market, which for authors align with the topic of their book. Blog writing can go either way: write blogs and create a book from them or write the book and blog about the topic to promote the book and gain followers.

One of the primary ways to promote a book these days is to be a "guest blogger" and do it during a, concentrated time period, and guest post on numerous blogs. This is called a "Virtual Book Tour," because you write for other people's blogs all across the Internet; thus the "tour." Schedule these "guest" appearances for each day of a one to three week period. Write the articles, ask the blog owners to post them on the appointed day, and then, write blogs for your own blog for the duration of your "book tour," which promotes the blog of the day!

Simple? Right! Another aspect of promoting your "Virtual Book Tour" is to get people to follow you from blog to blog. For this job, use a "Press Release" to announce your tour and gain interest. While" Press Releases" have been around for quite some time, a lot of people are not sure how to use them or how to write them. Take a deep breath in and out, relax, "Press Releases" are not that difficult. They generally answer these questions: who, what, where, when, why, and how, plus they usually are "Benefit-Driven." Tell your "story" in your "Press Release" while answering the questions. Make it as interesting as you possibly can, draw the reader into the story. And don't forget to post your "Press Release" to your Website with a link on your Media page.

For more information about Internet Marketing, check out this blog site more. "Bookmark It" or "Follow It" for more learning!

DAY 7 – WHY AUTHORS NEED TO LEARN HOW TO MARKET ONLINE
Guest Blog
by Connie Dunn

Authors need to learn how to "Market Online," because that's how books are sold these days. Some people still go to book stores, but we know from seeing big bookstores closing their locations that more and more people are buying books online. And while there are bookstores around, more and more people seek to learn about books online! So how do authors sell their books online?

Marketing a book and marketing a product are very similar in nature. For a product launch, you need to get a lot of buzz going. The same thing needs to happen for books!

Book authors need to know how to optimize blogs, Facebook, Twitter, LinkedIn, Google+, and other social media. They also need to know how to create a "Book Trailer," which is video marketing. One of the tried and true methods of selling a book online is done through what is called a Virtual Book Tour, which takes the author to a series of blogs where they have created a "guest blog" for their host site. The guest blog is written for the host site, which may not directly involve the topic of the book for which the author is promoting. However, the signature on the blog will be explicit and take the reader via a link to their book page or book site.

Social Media and Blog Writing are two important skills to have when setting up a Virtual Author Tour or Virtual Book Tour. Blogs are essential!

Blogs are simply short articles of 250-400 words. To get the most out of them, they should contain a keyword or keyword phrase in both the title and the first sentence. To learn more about "Internet Marketing," which includes both "Blog Writing," and "Social Media," look around this blog site and read more. For more learning, bookmark it or follow this blog!

DAY 8 – PUBLISH A BOOK TO PROMOTE YOUR BUSINESS
Guest Blog
by Connie Dunn

Publish a book to promote your business. There are three basic ways to use a book as a leveraging point in your business. The first is to publish a free e-book to give away when people sign up for your mailing list. It works to attract people to sign up, because they need the information in your "free book." This book should have content, but it should not be the sum total of the knowledge that you impart to your clients or customers. You can also have this book printed at one of the on-demand printer publishers so that you can use it as a business card at networking events.

The" Business Card" book is a good marketing tool when networking, because while people will throw out business cards, they tend to give away a book or keep it around. This means your marketing lives longer on someone's shelf or desk!

The second promotional book is referred to as a "First Encounter." It is a good tool for getting leads. The focus of this sort of book is to take one problem for which you solve and write about that topic. To get the most from this sort of e-book (either .pdf or Kindle, etc.) put in links to articles and other material, such as audio recordings, videos, or interviews on your Website. Sell this book for a low price, such as $5. Asking people to pay for this book, raises its credibility. Make sure to title the book in a way that it is obvious what problem it will solve!

The third type of promotional book is one that positions you as a "LEADER!" This book gives you the credentials that you need to move to the top of your industry. The topic in this sort of book needs to be the core or "signature" of your business. Since this book deals with the very cornerstone of what you do, it needs to be a longer book (up to 300 pages) and should sell at $20/book. This can be an e-book or a print book or offered in both formats. You should invest enough time and money in creating this book that it not only has compelling content but a selling cover, as well. This book should exude professionalism.

DAY 9 – INDEPENDENT PUBLISHERS MEET INDEPENDENT BOOKSTORES
Guest Blog
by Connie Dunn

"Independent Publishers" meet "Independent Bookstores" for a match that must have been made in "Book Heaven!"

With the big box bookstores like Borders going under and others closing locations don't be afraid that bookstores are becoming extinct! No, quite the contrary! We are reverting back to the "Ma and Pa" days of independently run bookstores. No two are alike. What a concept!

These stores tend to be quite a bit smaller with a smaller inventory, but they bring a unique friendliness about them. I love walking into places, such as Ugly Dog Books in

Attleboro, Massachusetts, where you browse, converse, and even bring your kids to story time with an Ugly Dog puppet who keeps you company!

As an "Indie" author and publisher, I have made it my mission to seek out small independent book stores. I know I haven't devoted as much time to this as I'd like, but there's always tomorrow.

For published authors, independent bookstores are much more willing to take your book and put it on their shelves. You become partners with these bookstores. The books are on consignment, so it doesn't cost the bookstore to keep it on the shelf. You gain because each time a different bookstore takes your book, you have another opportunity to sell your book.

As a consumer, independent bookstores bring you more diversity in book selections, because they do partner with authors. Most of the time, these authors are local people, which makes it even more unique. Sometimes, you even get to meet them and purchase a signed copy during a book signing event.

It's a win-win for everyone: consumer, author, and bookstore owner. Take a walk on the independent side and check out your local independent bookstore and discover American enterprise is well and strong!

DAY 10 – On this day, the Tour went to Amazon Author Central to see my site there and my Book Trailer for Press Releases Made Easy.

DAY 11 – MONEY AND THE BOOK WRITER
Guest Blog
by Connie Dunn

People write books for a variety of reasons. In my classes (publishwithconnie.com), I ask my students to define what they want to get from writing their book. While logical thinking says, "book writers want money," it isn't the only reason people write books. Some of those reasons are: desire to show a parent or other important relative their accomplishment; to tell their story; gain notoriety or credential; or to help other people. Understanding the relationship with their book helps them understand their relationship with money.

The "starving artist" too often applies to book writers. However, when the writer understands what experience they want to have as a result of writing their book, they can better understand what monetary remuneration that they wish to have. Naturally, to make money, the writer also has to understand how to market their book.

Learning the details of marketing can be rather fun. The newest method of marketing includes creating a "Virtual Book Tour," which includes writing articles for "guest blog" spots. This can be quite enjoyable. "Press Releases" are used to promote the "Tour," and then, you will hopefully begin to make money.

Passive income, such as that from a book, allows you to make money while you sleep…and that's the best sort of income to make! Do the work once, and continue making money. Every business person needs to include passive streams of income into their business plan. One of the easiest ways to do that is through book sales.

If you have a business and you are writing a book to establish a passive stream of income, you may find that the process gets easier and easier. Some books, of course, are more valuable as "free" incentives. It is the wise professional who can determine which one is which. That wise person can also repeat the process of writing a book for the purpose of creating a passive stream of income. Success for most folks lies in their ability to create multiple streams of income.

Book writers, like almost everyone, have relationships with money. It just needs to take on the mindset of making loads of money fast or a steady stream vs drips of cash or dried up assets.

DAY 12 – PASSION AND THE INDIE WRITER
Guest Blog
by Connie Dunn

"Passion and the indie writer" continues to amaze me. I teach people to write, publish, and market their books as independent publishers. For most of my writing students, writing is not a full-time career, but they are passionate about it. They work hard on their writing, and I encourage them to continue.

I've been writing all of my life. Given an array of opportunities to do whatever I want, writing always comes to the top. It's my passion. I also like to make puppets. Sometimes the writing and the making of puppets have come together. I made puppets to go with a children's story and illustrated it with the puppets.

Passion is one of those ingredients that you cannot help a writer develop. I can help them develop skills, teach them how to foreshadow and drop breadcrumbs throughout a story, and even create multiple plots. It's the passion, however, that comes through in the writing to create a magical and authentic flavor. The passion is something a writer brings to their story, which we see come through their characters.

Excitement isn't as easy as using words that a thesaurus can give you, it's the feeling that comes through the writing. If we could harness that sort of passion and put it into a pill, we would probably become millionaires. As it is, passion is an internal thing, a strong or intense emotion. When we tap into that well of emotional affinity, we can do just about anything, including a making a million dollars or more.

DAY 13 – PRESS REEASES: MARKETING SECRET STILL GOOD IN THE DIGITAL WORLD
Guest Blog Post
by Connie Dunn

Press Releases are a "Marketing Secret" that is still good in the "Digital World!" The Press Release is a tool to use for most anything that is happening in your business, such as new programs, product releases, and book launches. While you used to have to snail mail your Press Release to everyone on your news release mailing list, these days most publications accept them via e-mail.

While the Who, What, Where, When, Why, and How are the basics of any press release, there are ways to enhance your release. The way to get your press release noticed is to make it stand out.

Yes, you could use wild colored paper to make it stand out, but since you are no longer snail mailing the paper color won't matter. Sending it out through your e-mail, you could add a "stationary" background on some e-mail clients. However, this simply makes your file bigger and it could get deleted instead of read!

What a publication will notice is the words on your press release. Your Headline needs to be clear, yet grab attention. Using a few storytelling techniques, such as creating a good hook, can help your press release get read. Depending on the publication and the reason that you are sending a press release, writing your story within the press release can help get the message in print.

Newspaper journalists normally have a lot of articles to write. However, if they are also in charge of the whole page, which is often the case, they sometimes find the page needs more copy. They are not so likely to go out and do another story, but grabbing your well-written press release means they can just pop it into a blank spot with just a little editing for length.

Sending out press releases does not guarantee any publication will run it, but it may get it to the top of the stack! Then when there is opportunity, it may get printed! With news releases that are hooked to events that will pass, make sure to get them out well in advance. Sending one at the last minute or after it has passed will almost always guarantee that it ends up in their "circular" file.

DAY 14 – EDITING IS AN IMPORTANT STEP IN THE PUBLISHING PROCESS
Guest Blog
by Connie Dunn

Editing is an important step in the publishing process. While some writers invest a lot of time and effort into their writing process, it is equally important to invest in the editing process. Editing, however, should be done by an editing professional.

There are two major forms of editing: line editing or copy editing; and content or developmental editing. Line editing is the most common and is required for each manuscript. As the writer, it is difficult to find your own mistakes, because as you read, you read it like it should be rather than how it really is. This means that you miss errors, which are easily corrected.

Developmental, comprehensive, or content editing is a specialized form of editing that deals not with the grammar, spelling, and punctuation but the actual content. Some writers have difficulty in organizing their material to flow well. This mostly happens with non-fiction; however, it could happen in any genre.

Through content editing, material is reorganized into logical chapters. Often, the chapters themselves must be juggled to make the information flow logically. If chapters were not developed, these will be created and chunks of text will be moved into those chapters. Often writers have good knowledge of a topic, but are not able to convey it appropriately to its audience. This is when content editing comes into play.

Even after content editing, a manuscript needs to be copy or line edited to catch any mistakes. Common errors are usually in misspelling and happen in obvious places, such as the title or subtitle of your book. It's not that you are sloppy; you simply see it as it should be rather than how it really is. This is why editing is such an important process in publishing your book.

While getting a book published involves more than writing and editing, without these two processes, there really isn't a book! Other processes involve book design and formatting; cover design; publishing or getting the manuscript through the online process of the on-demand printer or publisher; and marketing, which can take quite some time in planning and executing.

DAY 15 – ORGANIZING IS MORE THAN A STATE OF MIND
Guest Blog
by Connie Dunn

Organizing is more than a state of mind. For example, we usually considered personality traits as giving us the ability to being an organized or disorganize person. While state of mind is not actually rooted in our personality, we often dub people's "modus operandi" as such.

There are many ways to organize. For example, writers must organize information, thoughts, and ideas. They may not organize physical things, such as paper, magazines, and such as well as they organize the intangible items like ideas. Being a writer is synonymous with being organized. No one reads a disorganized book!

Fortunately, organizing both the tangible and intangible are skills that can be learned. It is also helpful to know that cleaning out the clutter in your physical space often helps you become more organized in your mental and spiritual self.

Holistic healers tell us that our mental, spiritual, and physical beings are related. Holistic practices often heal our emotional being to heal our physical and spiritual being. Likewise, healing our spiritual self can also produce similar results on our physical and mental selves. We are beings of energy. Things and stuff, in general, are also energy. Because these are energy, they have the ability to siphon energy from other energy sources, which is what happens when we live in clutter.

Learning how to organize ourselves on all levels helps us become better at whatever we do. Writers and artists often want to exclude themselves from being affected by clutter, but the reality shows us differently.

We all need to learn how to become better organizers.

DAY 16 – WHY DO AUTHORS NEED TO LEARN ABOUT PRESS RELEASES, BLOGS, AND WEB DESIGN?

Guest Blog
by Connie Dunn

To market your book effectively, you need to learn how to write a good press release, write compelling blog articles, and design a Website that supports your best marketing efforts.

Press Releases need to start your marketing launch by announcing your events to the widest and most appropriate publications. Understanding your target market helps you know what publications that you want to target. Of course, sending a press release is not a guarantee that it will get published. For this reason, writing a press release that is stellar will put your release at the top of the stack.

Blogs are the basis for a good book marketing plan. You'll be writing guest blogs during a "Virtual Book Tour," which means you will visit a lot of blogs around the Web that speak to the topic of your book. Blog articles should be between 400-800 words. While the goal is to promote your book, you may find that some of your hosts may not directly relate to your book's topic. If this happens, then you will need to slant your article to suit the target audience of the blog you are visiting.

At the end of your post, include your signature which will direct people to your book page or blog. It should also incorporate your photograph and your book's cover. Get creative in designing your signature, which will go at the bottom of each guest blog.

Include in the design of your book, or author's Website some specific pages that will support your "Virtual Book Tour". Obviously, you need a page on your Website that summarizes your book. You also need these pages:

- Bio
- Contact information
- Events, including speaking engagements and your stops on your "Virtual Book Tour
- Endorsements

- Media, which needs to have your picture, a bio, a summary of your book, and a picture of your cover
- Blog, which will also have a blog post to promote each day's stop on your "Virtual Book Tour."

Do include an Opt-In, to allow persons to receive a Free Report, or E-Book. This will help you build your database of contacts or your list.

The design of your Website's Header should include your picture and your book cover. If the site is more of an author site, rather than a book site, then a graphic representing all your books would be more appropriate than a single book. The colors, graphics, etc. is all part of your branding.

Bringing together the three pieces of Press Releases, Blogs, and Web Design will do much to extend the reach of your marketing campaign.

DAY 17 – RE-WRITING YOUR LIFE STORY
Guest Blog
by Connie Dunn

Re-writing your life story can help you re-discover your "magnificent" self. Writing is a very broad brush that we can use in a variety of ways. While writing a book or a blog can work in some situations, the idea of re-writing your life story is quite different.

What happens in our lives can often wall us into a corner or, at the very least, a place in which we don't want to stay. Getting out of where we are takes some re-visioning or re-writing. As a writing coach, I mostly deal in issues surrounding the writing, publishing, and marketing processes; however, the coach side of me knows that re-writing our own life story is a powerful tool in helping us transform our lives.

What's remarkable is that no matter where our life has taken us, we can re-write the outcome to take us wherever our dreams and imagination can envision! Obviously, if you are reading this article, you will know that this is Barbara Wasserman's blog site. She has graciously agreed to allow me to guest blog on her site as part of a Virtual Blog Tour of my book, "Press Releases Made Easy," which has nothing to do with coaching and making life changes. However, in some situations, you might have use of writing a press release. Writing, on the other hand, knows no boundaries!

Writing can be done for professional or recreational purposes. My path has taken me through being a religious educator among other things, as a result I am aware of the power that writing has in change lives. We can write out our visions for our lives and come back to it over and over, re-write it, and again vision and re-vision to write and re-write our life's story. If there is one truth that I could impart here, it is that our lives are full of change. While "change" often seems difficult, reality is that life is full of oscillation and transformation!

Vision your most "magnificent" self, and write down your experiences and your visions for the future.

DAY 18 – THE THREE TOP REASONS FOR SUCCESSFUL BUSINESSES TO WRITE A BOOK
Guest Blog
by Connie Dunn

The three top reasons for successful businesses to write a book are: (1) to use as a network marketing tool; (2) to introduce what you do; and (3) to promote yourself as an expert.

Using a book as a network marketing tool allows you to stand out from the crowd. Because unlike business cards, books are not so easily thrown out, people tend to keep them around. They often end up floating around the office, which works well for marketing purposes! This book can also be used as an e-book to entice people to join your mailing list.

How do you introduce what you do now? You may have a variety of spiels and maybe even a brochure or two, but how much more impressive it would be to let your client or customer know you have a book that addresses his "specific" problem. You can have more than one book, but each book needs to address one specific problem. Charge a nominal fee, such as $5, so that the customer or client understands there is a value to what you are saying. Usually, the client is so blown away that you've addressed their problem, they hire you on the spot. Make sure the quality of the content is good, as well.

It isn't always easy to climb to the top of your field. There is some stiff competition to overcome. However, one way to stand out is to be a book author. While the previous types of books were ones where we wanted to limit the content so as not to give away the store, in this book you want to go deep into leveraging your core knowledge. Giving your readers what you give to clients and customers every day: the meaty breadth of your signature program. This book should be 80 to 300 pages and sell for $20.

These three different book types help your business grow, remember that delivering quality content is important in each of these.

DAY 19 – The Tour on this day visits Radio SOMA 1320 (soma1320.com) to listen to an interview.

DAY 20- - DELEGATING IS AN ESSENTIAL TOOL FOR A WRITER
Guest Blog
by Connie Dunn

Delegating is an essential tool for a writer. Writing can be all-encompassing, but some of us also have other aspects of our career. Therefore, delegating is even more important.

It is easy as solopreneurs just to continue to push on and do all of the work, when hiring a Virtual Assistant, for example, would raise the quality of the work and add some valuable time into your schedule. You might not use that time for work but rather spend it on self-care or with the family. Don't forget self-care, because burning the candle at both ends can be dangerous. I know that first hand!

Don't stop at considering a virtual assistant, there are other virtual services to be had! Anything from research to book marketing is available. Delegating some tasks to other people can be a healthy outlook for you and your business, whether it's book writing or involves services related to books or just other business endeavors.

I've found that women are often more reluctant to delegate. This may link back to our "super-mom" syndrome or our mistaken belief that we can multitask. While it is possible to multitask, what normally happens is that neither task is done with our peek quality. Maybe holding a kid on one hip and vacuuming works, but when we get to two kids, we don't have any hands to push the vacuum!

"Knowing our limits" is when we understand our potential. So…write that book, but think about delegating some pieces of it to someone else. Check out this Website, Castle

Virtual Solutions, for some good choices for delegating pieces of your book writing, publishing, and marketing.

DAY 21 – The Tour ends at www.conniedunnbooks.com/blog/ with a Trivia Contest.

Promotional Blogs Written for ConnieDunnBooks for Tour, July 1-21, 2013

VIRTUAL BOOK TOUR – DAY 1

Today, I am visiting the Dream Factory Community at www.dreamfactorycommunity.com.

My Guest Blog title is "How a Community can Support a Virtual Book Tour." One reason that I have chosen to start my Virtual Book Tour here is that this community has been very integral into my success as a Book Coach and my business, Publish with Connie, (www.publishwithconnie.com). They have also supported me by purchasing books, which are available at www.conniedunnbooks.com/books/.

Nancy Cantor, who is the founder of the Dream Factory Community and Cantor Consulting sparked my Publish with Connie and the Book Coaching business. I had a coaching session with her when she asked the question that had been hanging in the back of my head: "Why aren't you teaching people to write books?"

I had a lot of resistance to setting myself up as a writer, because after 9-11, my freelance writing community evaporated along with my marriage. Fortunately, Nancy was so excited by the idea of my becoming a Book Coach, it would have been hard not to have done this. Of course, I didn't do it for Nancy! I knew all along that what I was doing was writing. No matter what business endeavor I dabbled into, I was really just writing. While all my "unsuccessful" ideas were interesting, only the Book Coaching was supported by all my professional activities

I have been writing all my life. I self-published a cookbook in the 1980s, and went on to publish a few others until I began writing curricula for my church's religious education program. It was then, that I jumped into publishing e-courses and e-books!

I'm fortunate as a writer, because I always have several projects going and have never been left staring at a blank screen. It doesn't always go that smoothly for my clients, but I have some fool-proof methods to help them deal with that and just about every other issue that arises in publishing e-books, print books, and course materials (both e-courses and e-books).

I am a big proponent of "indie" publishing, which a lot of folks would call self-publishing. Self-Publishing and "Vanity Presses" have definitely tarnished the idea of self-publishing. The only thing you need is a "Publisher" or "Press" business name to use for publishingyou're your books. Then, you are an "Indie" or Independently Published author! Like the "Indie" movie business, "Indie" book publishing is on the rise.

I like teaching people of all ages to write and publish their books. In fact, I love it so much that I volunteered to teach children at the Attleboro (MA) library. The young adults (primarily 7th graders) were so talented! We're putting together an anthology of short stories and poetry.

I hope you enjoy following me on my tour…and…did I mention that there were prizes available? A trivia survey on Day 21 will determine the winners. For more information about this trivia contest, go to http://conniedunnbooks.com/events/trivia-contest/.

VIRTUAL BOOK TOUR – DAY 2

Today, I'm visiting the Hall of Fame for Virtual Book Tours at http://digitalpublishingcafe.com/virtual-book-tour-celebration-of-connie-dunn-author-of-press releases-made-easy/.

The Hall of Fame was designed by D'vorah Lansky as a way to honor people who had completed her course on Virtual Book Tours. The requirement was to complete the action items for each module. This actually had you creating a Website for your book tour with specific pages with specific content. A Blog was part of the Website, which meant that you needed to have posted some blogs. Since this is a Virtual "Blog" Tour (another name for the Virtual Book Tour), the blog becomes an important marketing tool. The blog is integral part of my "Tour," and marketing my book, "Press Releases Made Easy" (www.conniedunnbooks.com/books/press-releases-made-easy/).

D'vorah Lansky is a rare jewel of a teacher. Not only does she have great material herself, she brings in other professionals that give you a bigger picture of the world of

Book Marketing Online! One of her gifts is in honoring her students: thus, the Hall of Fame. She also has "Celebrity Author" status, check that out at http://becomeacelebrityauthor.com/.

Being in the Hall of Fame and getting "Celebrity Author" status is an honor. It makes me think that my students work hard, as well, but I have not yet developed any award program for them. So...students, tell me what you think! Obviously, these titles are taken!

Thank you for following me on my Virtual Book Tour, remember there are 19 more days!

VIRTUAL BOOK TOUR – DAY 3

Today is Day 3 of my Virtual Book Tour. Today I am writing about the "Heart Chakra and Book Writing" on my good friend, Helen Chin Lui's blog, located at http://www.healingplacemedfield.com/helen-chin-lui-certified-reflexologist-blogs.

Writing from your heart is a good way to write. There are many reasons to write in this way. One, of course, is to access your more spiritual and heart-centered self. Finding your spiritual or heart-center is a good way to begin writing, whether you are writing something you hope to sell, such as a book, or something strictly for yourself.

Helen Chin Lui is not only a top-notch reflexologist, which I would highly recommend; she is also an author. I suffer from psoriatic arthritis and some digestive issues. Helen works on my pain and digestive issues. I am on maintenance at this point, and only come in for reflexology about once a month.

Helen is one of my students and has recently published a children's book entitled: "Through My Mommy's Bellybutton," which is a delightful story written from the point of view of the baby in the belly. This is a "Must Have" book for any expectant mother. Her book can be found on Amazon.com.

My book, "Press Releases Made Easy," is a book that any entrepreneur needs if they are trying to do their own marketing. Sending out press releases to publications is a way of getting some "Free" marketing in the form of a newspaper article.

Authors who are also trying to do their own marketing should send out a Press Release to announce their Virtual Book Tour! Check out my Press Release at http://www.conniedunnbooks/Press Release - Virtual Book Tour.pdf

VIRTUAL BOOK TOUR – DAY 4

Today is Day 4 of my Virtual Book Tour. Today, we will visit http://www.publishwithconnie.com, which is my other Website for my education courses for learning how to write, publish, and market your book.

When you begin marketing your book, there are many aspects to examine. A Virtual Book Tour, such as this is a good way to market a book. I am promoting my book: "Press Releases Made Easy," which can be found at http://www.conniedunnbooks.com/book/press-releases-made-easy/

This post is about marketing and how press releases fit into a book marketing plan. See my Press Release: http://www.conniedunnbooks/Press Release - Virtual Book Tour.pdf

VIRTUAL BOOK TOUR – DAY 5

Today is Day 5 of my Virtual Book Tour. Today, I am visiting my friend, Janet Parnes' Website at http://etiquettefortoday.net/blog/ for my Guest Blog: "Etiquette of a Virtual Book Tour."

Janet, as you may surmise, is an etiquette specialist. She uses the terms "first impression" and "etiquette expert." Her clients include children, youth, and young adults. From job interview skills to life skills to learning polite behaviors, Janet covers it.

First impressions in the business world are so important that if you don't make a good impression, you probably won't be doing business with that person or their firm. However, more and more transactions are done online, and so the impression you make happens in impersonal communications, such as e-mail. The virtual world is here to stay, perhaps we need to redefine some of our business etiquette.

Learning how to do a Virtual Book Tour also contains some simple business etiquette. In all our work relationships, we should be aware of the polite behavior that becomes professionals, and follow best etiquette practices.

VIRTUAL BOOK TOUR – DAY 6

Today is Day 6 of my Virtual Book Tour. Today, we will visit my friend, Ed McDonough's Blog, at http://www.executivecoachingbusinessblog.com/. Ed is an Internet Marketing Specialist. My guest blog is entitled: "Book Marketing Using Blogs and Press Releases."

Ed is not just my friend, but is also my marketing specialist. I recommend him highly. He is very skilled in writing marketing copy and creating videos for marketing purposes. Ed and I are collaborating on a book about book marketing. With my classes from D'vorah Lansky (I spoke about this on Day 2) on Virtual Book Tours, I may actually have something to contribute, especially, since I am taking my own Virtual Book Tour.

One of the things that I've learned from Ed is that you have to continue learning. Marketing used to be a strategy that used a combination of print ads, press releases, radio and television advertising, and the juggling of a lot of marketing and demographic data. Now days, most marketing is played out online, and it needs to involve social media.

Changes in the way we do business have been influenced by the developments of technology. Marketing makes use of audio, video, and visual opportunities. On most laptops, any individual can easily harness the power of these technologies to create their own marketing power house.

Press Releases continue to be a valuable part of marketing tools, even though they have been around since the beginning of the newspaper industry. "Press Releases Made Easy" can help you make use of this tool. To read more about this book, go to http://conniedunnbooks.com/books/press-releases-made-easy/. To see more about the Virtual Book Tour, check out our Events at http://conniedunnbooks.com/events. And don't forget to check out our day's stop at http://www.executivecoachingbusinessblog.com/ and check out more of Ed's Website!

VIRTUAL BOOK TOUR – DAY 7

Today is Day 7 of my Virtual Book Tour. Again, I will be traveling to a friend's Blog Site. I'd like to introduce you to Dave Miles at http://milesinternetmarketing.com/blog/. My Guest Blog title is "Authors Need to Learn How to Market Online."

Dave says that he "redirects customers from your competition to your site." That's a great marketing statement, and Dave actually does this through a number ways, including: 1) a Website that is designed to be the Hub of all your online activities; 2) Website design that works for Mobile Phones (this is just now coming into its own, make sure your site works for mobile users); 3) reputation marketing (Dave is the only marketing professional that I know who does this) works by checking out reviews of your business, adding 5-star reviews, and eliminating bad reviews; 4) high-ranking video ads; 5) optimizing Google+ local places; 6) use Google Adwords Campaigns (this is a low-cost for high visibility option); 7) flexible QR codes can be used and repurposed with the same QR code for a variety of marketing tasks; 8) custom Facebook timelines; and 9) connecting your business Facebook Page to your Pinterest account.

I put Dave in a category above most people, because not only does he do a lot for you in his marketing services, he's just a great guy! He's an authority on the many forms of Internet Marketing and he's willing to share some of his knowledge to those of us who only have our pinky toes in the marketing water.

So I definitely have to thank Dave for allowing me to guest blog on his site, because my knowledge of all things marketing can probably fit into a thimble in comparison to what Dave knows. Fortunately, I'm not competing with Dave. My marketing goals are to learn enough to leverage the sales of my own books and to teach other book writers to do the same. If you need more than that, well…Dave's the man to talk with! His website is http://milesinternetmarketing.com/. To view my guest blog, go to http://milesinternetmarketing.com/blog/.

VIRTUAL BOOK TOUR – DAY 8

Today is Day 8 of my Virtual Book Tour. Today, we will visit my friend, Ed Drozda's Blogsite at http://www.thewatertrough.typepad.com/. My Guest Blog is titled "Publish a Book to Promote Your Business."

Ed's Website is http://4eandd.com/. Ed is a small business coach. His philosophy is "Developing clarity around yourself is an essential step in achieving your goals. Many of us do not appreciate the need for this clarity and as a result we are not fully aware of the breadth of our potential."

As I work with book writers (www.publishwithconnie.com), I see his philosophy works for this population, as well. Many book writers don't realize that when they finish their book, they "ARE" in business! If it's a hobby, there's not as much reason to publish the book. Most authors and potential authors have their publishing goals fixed on the final published book.

Since through the simple act of printing your book, you find yourself in business, you may have a lot of questions. Ed is the person to talk with about setting up your business for success.

In my article "Publish a Book to Promote Your Business," I talk about how a "Free" book can help build your e-list or "Followers." Authors need to develop that list of people who want to purchase their books. Even though you aren't developing a list for newsletters, you still need to build the e-list. Newsletters will help you keep in touch with fans of your writing. If you have more than one book, I would start an author Website, so all your books are in one place instead of scattered all over the Web. For better clarity on that, contact a marketing professional.

However, if you need help in setting up your business, contact Ed Drozda, the small business doctor, who can help you find your way around the maze of business start-up headaches! His website address is http://4eandd.com/. Check out his blog at http://www.thewatertrough.typepad.com with my guest article "Publish a Book to Promote Your Business."

VIRTUAL BOOK TOUR – DAY 9

Today is Day 9 of my Virtual Book Tour. Today, we are going to Ugly Dog Books, an independent bookstore in Attleboro, MA. My friend, Kim Storch, is the owner. My guest blog "Independent Publishers Meet Independent Bookstores" can be found on the Ugly Dog Bookstore's Blog at http://uglydogbooks.com/blog.htm or http://uglydogbooks.blogspot.com/.

Kim Storch is a delightful woman, who is also the author of "Footprints in the Snow." She donates 10% of the proceeds of this book to the St. Joseph's Food Cellar. The bookstore carries new and used books. She also runs quite a few workshops and other events! One of the highlights at Ugly Dog Books is the Author of the Month and the Artist of the Month. She features the books and art in her store; and for authors, she schedules a "Book Signing" event.

Ugly Dog Books is a small independent book store with the mission of making it a comfortable place for people of all ages to come, sit, read, and shop. You will often find a bit of chatting, unique gift items and cards, as well as a large selection of books.

Children will enjoy the children's room. Used books in the kid's area are usually $1/softcover and $4/hardcover.

Checking out local independent bookstores takes us back to the days of the ma and pa run businesses. Next time you're visiting a new town, check them out! Drop me a line with their contact info, so I can see if they'd like to carry some indie books of mine and my many students!

Ugly Dog Books can be found at http://uglydogbooks.com/ and their blog is http://uglydogbooks.com/blog.htm with my guest article "Independent Publishers Meet Independent Bookstores."

VIRTUAL BOOK TOUR – DAY 10

Today is Day 10 of my Virtual Book Tour. Today, I am taking you to Amazon.com's Author Central at amazon.com/author/conniedunn. This is where information about authors resides. You should be able to watch my book trailer for "Press Releases Made Easy" from this location, as well.

The Author Central of Amazon.com helps readers learn more about the author. Many authors may have multiple videos for multiple books. I am relatively new to the idea of a "Book Trailer." Thus far, this is my only Book Trailer.

The ways in which authors can market their book are consistently changing as more and more options appear on the Internet.

Video Marketing is a huge success at this time. People aren't as interested in talking heads, but text and graphic based materials with voice overs are very important, so I am told by marketing gurus, such as Ed McDonough (www.executivecoached.com)

The best way to create a video is to start with a PowerPoint (part of Microsoft Office) Presentation. You can do some fancy animation with it or not. The power in PowerPoint is that you can move graphics and text around easily. You can rotate all items, as well. This gives you some interesting slides for your video. Put text on the pages, but you do not have to put all the text on the slides. You do need a script to make the audio sound better.

Animation and narration can be done within PowerPoint. You can also run the slides and use the capture feature available on many video editing programs. Powerpoint allows you to save a file as a Windows Media Video, which can be imported into most video editing software. You can edit long pauses out. Some programs will allow you to clean up the audio. To create a good audio track, use a microphone that attaches to the USB Port on your computer. You can use many utilities to convert your video into an MP4 file, if your video editing doesn't support rendering to an MP4.

I have found that PowerPoint is rather fun to create in. There are limits to its animation features, but it still creates some interest on otherwise dull text pages.

If you use other programs to create slide shows, check out their features. You still might be able to do some of the same ideas I've discussed in this Blog. Don't forget to check out Amazon Author Central at amazon.com/author/conniedunn.

VIRTUAL BOOK TOUR – DAY 11

Today is Day 11 of my Virtual Book Tour. Today, we are visiting my friend, Reva Kussmaul at her blog, http://moneyvisions.net/category/blog/, where my guest article "Money and the Book Writer" can be found.

Reva wears several hats, and today we're going to talk about her coaching business, "MoneyVisions." She helps people develop better relationships with money. It is easy to create bad relationships with money, such as the consistent spending of more than your income, which lands you into large credit card debt fast!

Reva, herself, found that she was under-earning and overspending, which saddled her with more than $120,000 of debt. Most people would be crushed by this situation. Instead, Reva, figured out for herself what needed to change. It was her relationship to money. She has since coached people to change their own relationship to money. She does this from the perspective of someone who learned first-hand. She says that she doesn't judge, but she does "compassionately kick your ass."

MoneyVisions provides education for business owners and individuals who need assistance in building a new relationship with money. It is founded upon principles of "purposeful prosperity." Reva is dedicated to changing the way others look at their money by empowering them to see their money with clarity, simplicity and purpose.

As book writers, the relationship with money needs to come into play. You can spend more than $20,000 getting your book published. However, if you have not only a right relationship with money but have done your research, you will find that maybe a few thousand to less than $100 is possible, depending on what services you have had to hire. I regularly point people in the right direction!

Self-publishing through Vanity Presses will cost you $20,000 and more. I don't know about you, but I don't have that kind of cash. And these fees are prior to marketing! To learn more about what I do for writers, go to www.publishwithconnie.com. To read my guest article, "Money and the Book Writer," go to http://moneyvisions.net/category/blog/. If you have large amounts of debt, contact Reva. Her Website is http://moneyvisions.net

VIRTUAL BOOK TOUR – DAY 12

Today is Day 12. Today, we will be visiting the blog of "The Millionaire Woman", Debra Kasowski, at http://debrakasowski.com/category/blog/. My guest blog is titled, "Passion and the Indie Writer."

Debra, The Millionaire Woman, coaches people to be "rich" from the inside out. Being a millionaire "is not just about the money," she says. "You do not need to sacrifice your priorities or values to get ahead."

Debra's focus is to help women and men to grow their business, raise their family and create a life they love. When coaching, she becomes a partner with her clients in helping them gain clarity and focus to build a strategic plan for getting wherever they want to get to in their life. She also helps people boost their credibility, increase their visibility in the marketplace, and attract more clients.

Becoming successful is not a passive endeavor, but Debra helps people work on both their abilities to compete in the world, as well as their desire and passion for life.

To read more about Debra Kasowski and The Million Dollar Woman, go to http://debrakasowski.com/. To read my guest blog post on "Passion and the Indie Writer," go to http://debrakasowski.com/category/blog/.

VIRTUAL BOOK TOUR – DAY 13

Today is Day 13 on my Virtual Book Tour. Today, we're visiting Marcia Ming's blog at http://savvymarketingsecrets.com/blog/ and my guest blog, "Press Releases: Marketing Secret Still Good in the Digital World."

Marcia Ming of Savvy Marketing Secrets is on a mission to help small businesses with their marketing by gathering up the most up-to-date marketing information, which tends to change just about every day.

However, to make sure that all your marketing questions are answered, Marcia invites you to e-mail the Savvy Marketing Secrets so that they can answer your questions. If you're struggling with an issue, chances are that hundreds of other businesses are experiencing the same.

The Savvy Marketing Secrets (http://savvymarketingsecrets.com) also has resources and product reviews. The Internet changed how we do business, including press releases. "Press Releases Made Easy," the book that I am promoting on my Virtual Book Tour, can be found at http://conniedunnbooks.com/books/press-releases-made-easy/. My Guest Blog on the Savvy Marketing Secrets can be found at http://savvymarketingsecrets.com/blog/.

VIRTUAL BOOK TOUR – DAY 14

Today is Day 14 of my Virtual Book Tour. We will be traveling to a new friend, Gina Akao's Blog at http:// writingandeditingtoday.com/blog/. My Guest Blog title is: "Editing Is an Important Step in the Publishing Process."

Gina is a writer and a professional editor, which is someone every writer needs to know! She is also a freelance writer and offers consulting services to authors and small business owners who need help with websites, blogs and social media management. Her book, "Tales of a Law School Dropout," is available on Amazon.com. Her author website is http://www.ginaakao.com.

Gina and I met in a class online, Virtual Book Tours, taught by D'vorah Lansky http://www.bookmarketingmadeeasy.com/. We are both featured on the Virtual Book Tour Hall of Fame at http://digitalpublishingcafe.com/celebrating-gina-akao-virtual-book-tour-hall-of-fame-achiever/ and http://becomeacelebrityauthor.com/virtual-book-tour-celebration-of-connie-dunn-author-of-press-releases-made-easy/.

You will also see her article posted yesterday, July 13, at http://www.publishwithconnie.com/blog for her Virtual Book Tour. My article "Editing Is an Important Step in the Publishing Process" discusses all the reasons you need a professional editor when editing your book. You may see this article at: http:// writingandeditingtoday.com/blog/

VIRTUAL BOOK TOUR – DAY 15

Today is Day 15 on my Virtual Book Tour. Today, we will be visiting Kazia Navas' blog at http:// writingandeditingtoday.com/blog/. My article title is "Organizing Is More than a State of Mind."

Kazia is one of my LinkedIn Contacts. LinkedIn reported "there were more than 175 million registered users of the site." LinkedIn is a gem of a place to develop contacts. It is primarily business-to-business, and people often keep their contacts within certain industries. However, as a writer and book coach, my contacts include people that I know or get to know from a broad brush stroke of industries.

When setting up my book tour, I looked for people that I already knew first. Secondly, I looked to my LinkedIn Contacts, because these are people that I also communicate with for professional and business reasons. While there is a school of thought that you should find people whose blogs are on the same topic as your book, I looked to broaden that out a bit. I just couldn't imagine writing 21 blogs about Press Releases. Although there are plenty of ideas within press releases to support multiple articles, I wanted people to follow me on my book tour. No one wants to read 21 blog articles about any one topic. So I thought I'd broaden out a bit.

Naturally, I felt like the topics needed to loosely connect with writing, which "ORGANIZING" does. You cannot write without some organizational skills. They may not translate into physical organization, but organizing your "thoughts and ideas" are an important ingredient in writing.

Kazia is a professional organizer. She is passionate about "helping people create more peaceful, and nurturing environments." She does this by understanding her clients, so she gets to know them and understands what is important to them. She, then, uses that knowledge to create workable systems and solutions for them. Her personalized service is what draws her clients.

Thank you Kazia for being open to my guest blogging on your blog at: http:// writingandeditingtoday.com/blog/. Go to her blog and read "Organizing Is More than a State of Mind."

VIRTUAL BOOK TOUR – DAY 16

Today is Day of 16 of my Virtual Book Tour. We will be traveling to Eunice Nisbett's blog today at http://www.savvyvirtuals.co/bookmarketing/blog/ for my guest blog, "Why Do Authors Need to Learn about Press Releases, Blogs, and Web Design?"

Eunice Nisbett is a new friend that I met through D'vorah Lansky's Virtual Book Tour Class (http://www.bookmarketingmadeeasy.com/category/virtual-book-tour/) and the writer's Facebook Group that accompanies that course. Eunice runs an online book marketing resource service. She encourages people to "take your book beyond boundaries." Her work helps authors become "best selling" authors.

Eunice will be the first to tell you that marketing your book online is not always easy. While there is a lot of technology that makes marketing easier and more affordable than it was even a decade ago, it may be too time-consuming for some busy authors and technology challenging for others. Eunice, however, will help you with any and all phases of your marketing. She encourages authors to take their book beyond borders and into the global, which the Internet allows. To learn more about Eunice Nesbitt and her book marketing services, go to http://www.savvyvirtuals.co/bookmarketing/http://www.savvyvirtuals.co/bookmarketing/.

You can read my guest blog at http://www.savvyvirtuals.co/bookmarketing/blog/.

VIRTUAL BOOK TOUR – DAY 17

Today is Day 17 of my Virtual Book Tour. We will be going to Barbara Wasserman's Coaching Blog at http://barbarawassermancoaching.com for my Guest Blog "Re-Writing Your Life Story."

Barbara Wasserman is one of my LinkedIn contacts. Recently, one of my friends asked me what she was really supposed to do with LinkedIn. It seems that she's been collecting contacts, but nothing else. While if you're into collecting contacts, it works, but what if you actually engage your contacts, talk to them through messages, and ask them to be a partner for something very small, such as hosting a guest blog. My purpose is to promote my book, "Press Releases Made Easy." Although the book topic and Barbara's site seem to be incongruent, I found my link was in "writing" and the fact that her coaching was to "empty nest women."

I had survived being an "empty nester." My youngest daughter has been out of my home for about five-and-a-half years. It was tough, because she was my youngest and my only birth child. She had basically been joined at my hip for 20 years, when she moved to South Carolina to be with her boyfriend. I wasn't enamored of her going so far away, especially since she has a heart condition. But life moves along whether we like it or not. I've moved on to write books and teach people to write their books.

Thanks to Barbara Wasserman for being part of my Virtual Book Tour. You can see my article, "Re-Writing Your Life Story," on her blog at http://barbarawassermancoaching.com.

VIRTUAL BOOK TOUR – DAY 18

Today is Day 18 on my Virtual Book Tour. We are visiting Kate Breeders' blog at http://www.successcoachingwithkate.com/blog/ for my guest blog, "The Three Top Reasons for Successful Businesses to Write a Book."

Kate Breeders and I actually have several connections: she's one of my LinkedIn contacts; she occasionally attends the Dream Factory Community luncheons, for which I am a member; and she knows one of my friends, Janet Parnes, who is an etiquette professional. Kate's big question for her clients is: "Are you ready to kick up your success and satisfaction to a whole new level?" If you are a procrastinator, go to Kate's site and get her free, "Procrastinator Buster Training" at http://www.successcoachingwithkate.com.

Kate's mission is: "To help people make the impossible, possible." Her business is all about success, and though the book that I am promoting is "Press Releases Made Easy," my guest article is "The Three Top Reasons for Successful Businesses to Write a Book." To read it, go to http://www.successcoachingwithkate.com/blog/.

VIRTUAL BOOK TOUR – DAY 19

Today is Day 19 on my Virtual Book Tour. Today, we will be traveling to SOMA Radio 1320 AM at http://www.soma1320.com. At this location, you can listen to an interview. Domenic (Dom) Cotoia interviewed me on his Early Morning Show on June 26. SOMA Radio 1320 is part of the Double ACCS (http://www.doubleaccs.com), the public access channels for Attleboro, MA. There are programs online that are shown live and then archived there for your perusal. I watched Emily's Garden, which I found very informative about the crafting of hooked rugs.

During my Interview with Dom, I talked about the Virtual Book Tour, my book, "Press Releases Made Easy," and other books found on Connie Dunn Books, http://www.conniedunnbooks.com/books/. I also talked about what I do as a Book Coach in helping people write, publish, and market their books at Publish with Connie (http://www.publishwithconnie.com).

This opportunity was fun! I am hoping to appear again on Dom's Early Morning Show. Don't forget to visit http://www.soma1320.com.

VIRTUAL BOOK TOUR – DAY 20

Today is Day 20 on my Virtual Book Tour. We are visiting Lorraine Castle's blog site at http://www.castlevirtualsolutions.com/blog/ for my guest blog "Delegating Is an Essential Tool for a Writer."

Lorraine Castle is a new friend that I met through D'vorah Lanky's course, "Virtual Book Tours Made Easy." Her company, Castle Virtual Solutions, provides virtual assistance to writers. She says, "I specialize in supporting writers and authors."

Her company provides coaching and mentoring services to new and established writers; research and fact checking; manuscript preparation for submission to the publisher; assist with book proposal; obtain ISBN, register copyright, and generate barcode; coordinate e-book process; coordinate virtual book launch using Amazon.com and other marketing vehicles; write and distribute press releases; format and distribute newsletters and announcements; and manage your social networking sites and your website.

My guest blog article is about delegating, because delegating is an excellent and essential tool for writers. Outsourcing some of the tasks involved in writing, publishing, and marketing your book can help you get to other more pressing tasks, such as beginning your next book!

To read my guest blog, go to http://www.castlevirtualsolutions.com/blog. Also check out all the services available from Castle Virtual Solutions.

Virtual Book Tour – Day 20

Today is Day 20 on my Virtual Book Tour. We are visiting Lorraine Castle's blog site at http://www.castlevirtualsolutions.com/blog/ for my guest blog "Delegating Is an Essential Tool for a Writer."

Lorraine Castle is a new friend that I met through D'vorah Lanky's course, "Virtual Book Tours Made Easy." Her company, Castle Virtual Solutions, provides virtual assistance to writers. She says, "I specialize in supporting writers and authors."

Her company provides coaching and mentoring services to new and established writers; research and fact checking; manuscript preparation for submission to the publisher; assist with book proposal; obtain ISBN, register copyright, and generate barcode; coordinate e-book process; coordinate virtual book launch using Amazon.com and other marketing vehicles; write and distribute press releases; format and distribute newsletters and announcements; and manage your social networking sites and your website.

My guest blog article is about delegating, because delegating is an excellent and essential tool for writers. Outsourcing some of the tasks involved in writing, publishing, and marketing your book can help you get to other more pressing tasks, such as beginning your next book!

To read my guest blog, go to http://www.castlevirtualsolutions.com/blog. Also check out all the services available from Castle Virtual Solutions.

VIRTUAL BOOK TOUR - DAY 21

Today is Day 21 of my Virtual Book Tour, which is the last day of my tour. Today, I am posting the Trivial Contest. The first one to e-mail me at conniedunnbooks@gmail.com with all 20 questions correct will receive a personalized and signed copy of any book on this site (http://www.conniedunnbooks/books/). The next 5 people to e-mail me with all 20 questions correct will receive a personalized and signed copy of" Press Releases Made Easy."

TRIVIA QUESTIONS

1. On Day 1, we visited the Dream Factory Community blog. The Dream Factory Community helps members succeed at their life, their _____, and their _____.

2. On Day 2, we visited the Virtual Book Tour Hall of Fame, where I am introduced. What is the name of the book that is no longer in print?

3. On Day 3, we visited Healing Place Medfield's blog. What is the name of the free report offered?

4. On Day 4, we visited my site Publish with Connie, name one of the Free e-book available if you sign up for my e-mail list?

5. On Day 5, we visited Etiquette for Today. What service is offered to college students?

6. On Day 6, we visited Executive Coaching Business Blog. What is the Internet Paradox?

7. On Day 7, we visited Miles Internet Marketing Blog. What is Reputation Marketing?

8 On Day 8, we visited The Water Trough Blog. What is the relationship between a "free e-book" and a "business card" book?

9. On Day 9, we visited Ugly Dog Books Blog. What day and time is storytime?

10. On Day 10, we visited Amazon Author Central (amazon.com/author/conniedunn) to watch the book trailer. How many books are on my page?

11 .On Day 11, we visited Money Visions Blog. Name one thing that brings in money while you sleep.
12. On Day 12, we visited Debra Kasowski, the Millionaire Woman, who will be taking her own Virtual Book Tour in September. What is the name of her book?

13. On Day 13, we visited Savvy Marketing Secrets Blog. Can you name three writers mentioned on this site?

14. On Day 14, we visited Writing and Editing Today/Blog. Name two types of editing.

15. On Day 15, we visited Organizing by Kazia/Blog. Clutter depletes time, _____ and _____.

16. On Day 16, we visited Savvy Best Sellers Blog. What is the name of the Newsletter?

17. On Day 17, we visited Barbara Wasserman Coaching/Blog. What sort of coach is Barbara?

18. On Day 18, we visited Success Coaching with Kate. Kate Breeder has a free course on _____.

19. On Day 19, we visited Radio Station SOMA 1320 AM on Facebook.com/soma1320/. What was Connie's first self-published book project?

20. On Day 20, we visited Castle Virtual Solutions/Blog. What are Virtual Solutions?

**Ta-Da!
And Now
the Money
Stacks Up!**

About the Author

Connie Dunn, owner of Publish with Connie and creator of *12 Easy Steps to Publishing*, is an author, speaker and educator.

She has more than 25 years of experience in writing for magazines and newspapers. She had a regular column in the Dallas Morning News, which focused on small and home-based businesses. She won an award from the SBA for the work she did in highlighting home-based businesses.

Connie also developed courseware for a number of start-up technology firms. She worked with publishers, such as Prentice Hall and Taylor Publishing as a Developmental (content) Editor. She self-published her first book in 1981, and developed a collection of stories with a collaborator in the 1990s. She writes children's books, non-fiction, and fiction.

Connie believes that everyone has a book in them. She wants to help you fulfill those valuable contributions of wisdom to the world that you have locked away in your mind. If you don't write it, no one will ever know the wisdom you have to share.

Connie's specialties are: independent publishing, and making book writing, publishing, and marketing easy. See her courses at http://www.publishwithconnie.com.

She started writing early and now has about 30 books, screen plays, and curricula published. She has taught creative writing, freelance writing, religious education, and a variety of creativity workshops. She writes children's books, non-fiction, and fiction.

See her books at http://www.conniedunnbooks.com.

And now. . . We're at the END!

www.ingramcontent.com/pod-product-compliance
Lightning Source LLC
Chambersburg PA
CBHW081200270326

41930CB00014B/3235